Hidden
in the Jungle

POSTER PAD

Sara Muzio

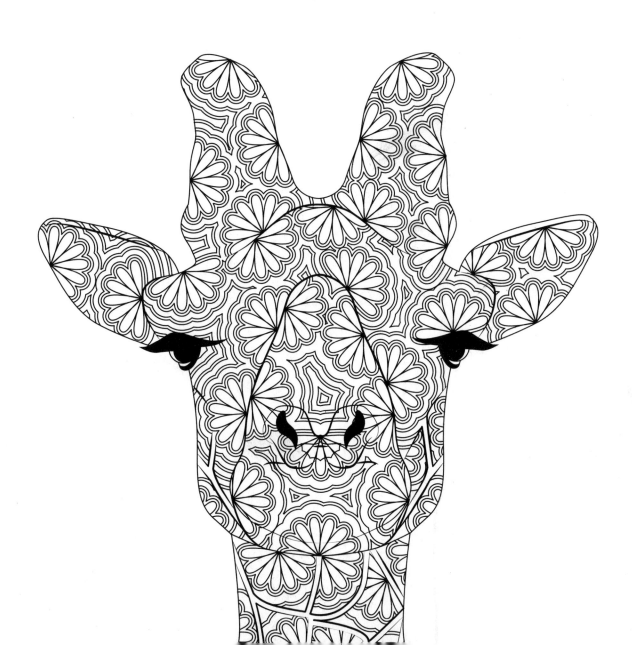

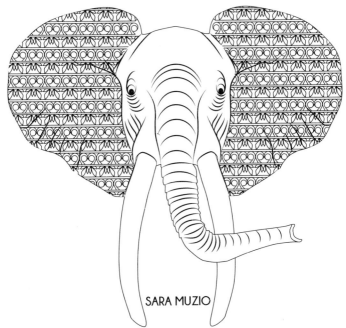

SARA MUZIO

Sara Muzio has over ten years of experience
working in graphic design and illustration.
In 2002, after earning a degree in Medical Illustration, she began working for small graphic
design studios and in 2004 she became the scientific illustrator for Lumen Edizioni, where
she completed a postgraduate course on publishing and advertising graphics.
From 2005 to 2011, Sara worked as a freelance graphic designer
for private clients as well as public entities and publishing houses.
From 2011 to 2013, she was the graphic and packaging
designer for Sambonet Paderno Industrie S.p.A.
She currently works as a freelance graphic designer and
as the Marketing Assistant for "La Salute nel Sale," a halotherapy
center with locations in Vercelli and Casale, Italy.
In addition to the illustrations found in this book, she created those
for *Flower Fantasy Poster Pad* for White Star Publishers.

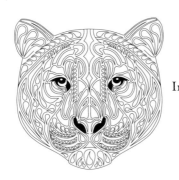

COVER GRAPHIC DESIGN
Michela Barbonaglia

GRAPHIC LAYOUT
Valentina Giammarinaro

TRANSLATION
ICEIGEO, Milan

New York

An Imprint of Sterling Publishing
1166 Avenue of the Americas
New York, NY 10036

ISBN 978-1-4547-0940-4

Distributed in Canada by Sterling Publishing
c/o Canadian Manda Group, 664 Annette Street
Toronto, Ontario, Canada M6S 2C8

For information about custom editions, special sales, and
premium and corporate purchases, please contact Sterling
Special Sales at 800-805-5489 or
specialsales@sterlingpublishing.com.

Manufactured in China

10 9 8 7 6 5 4 3

larkcrafts.com

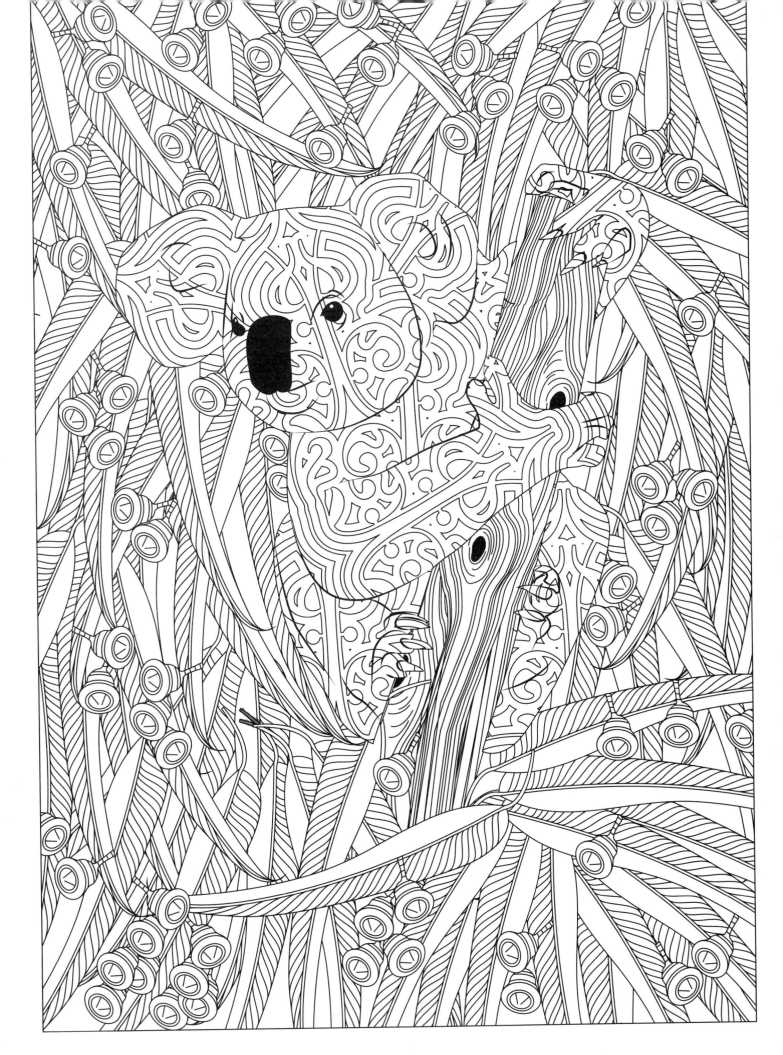

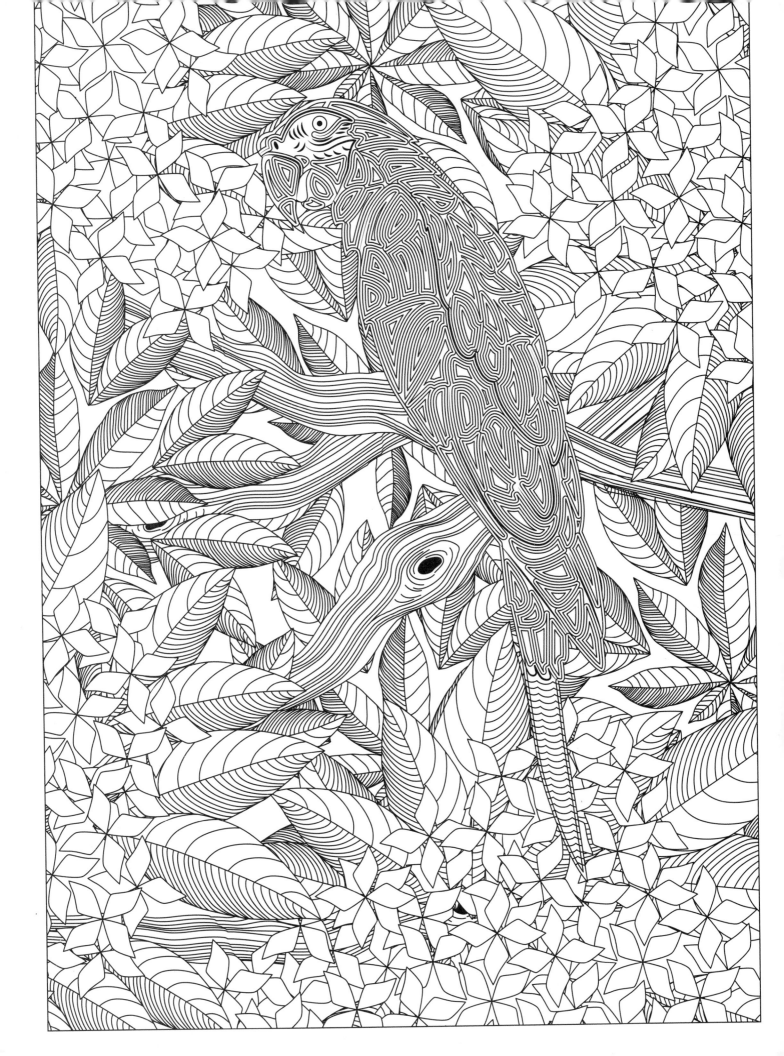

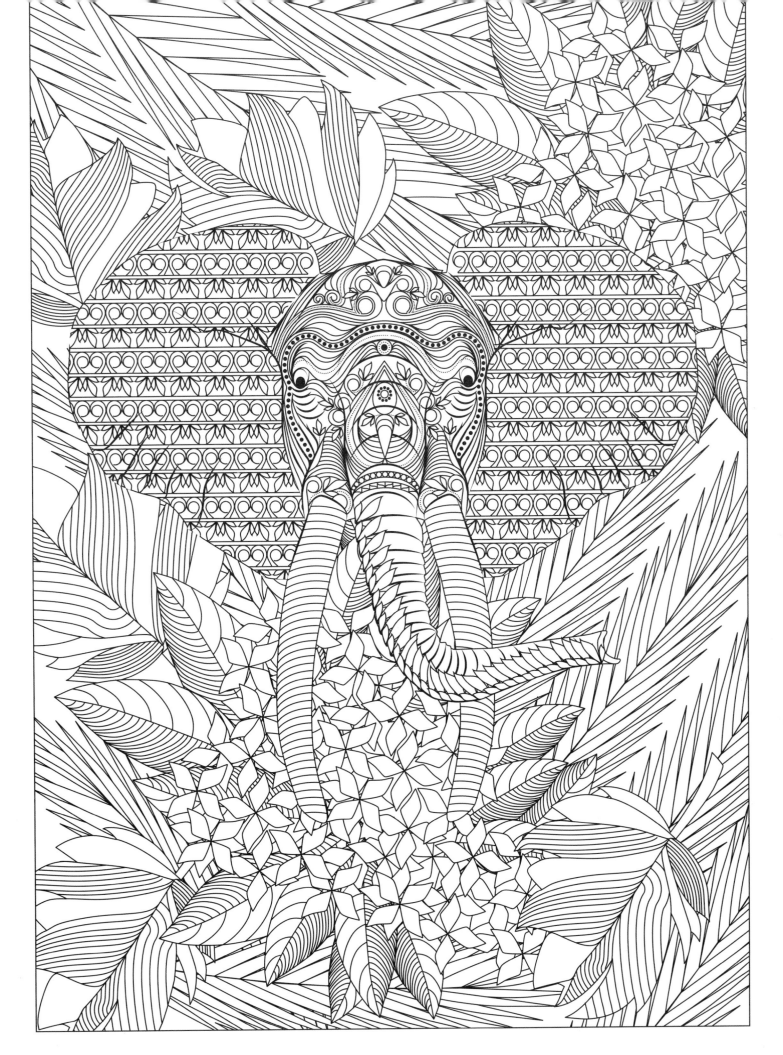

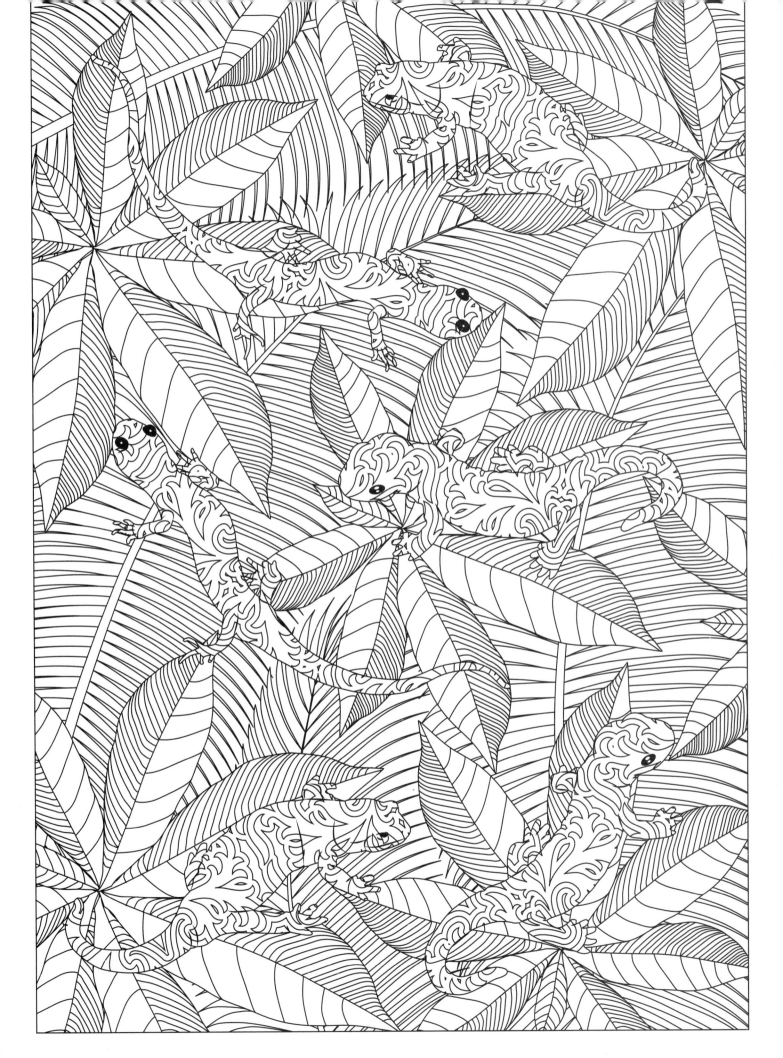

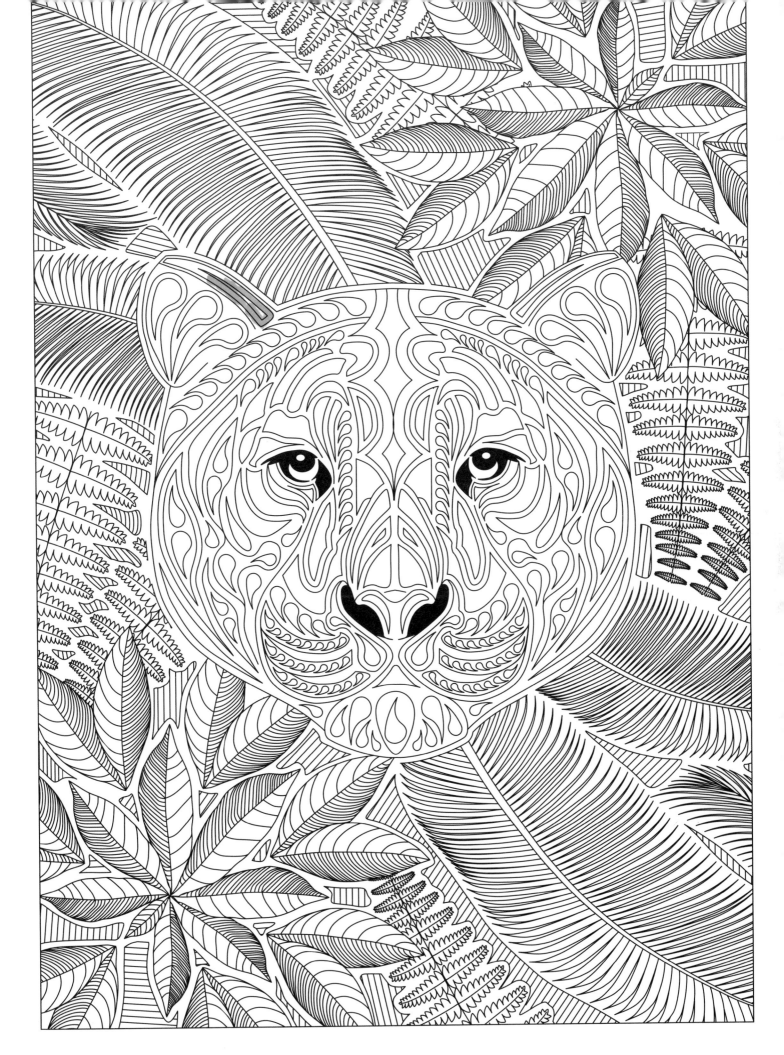

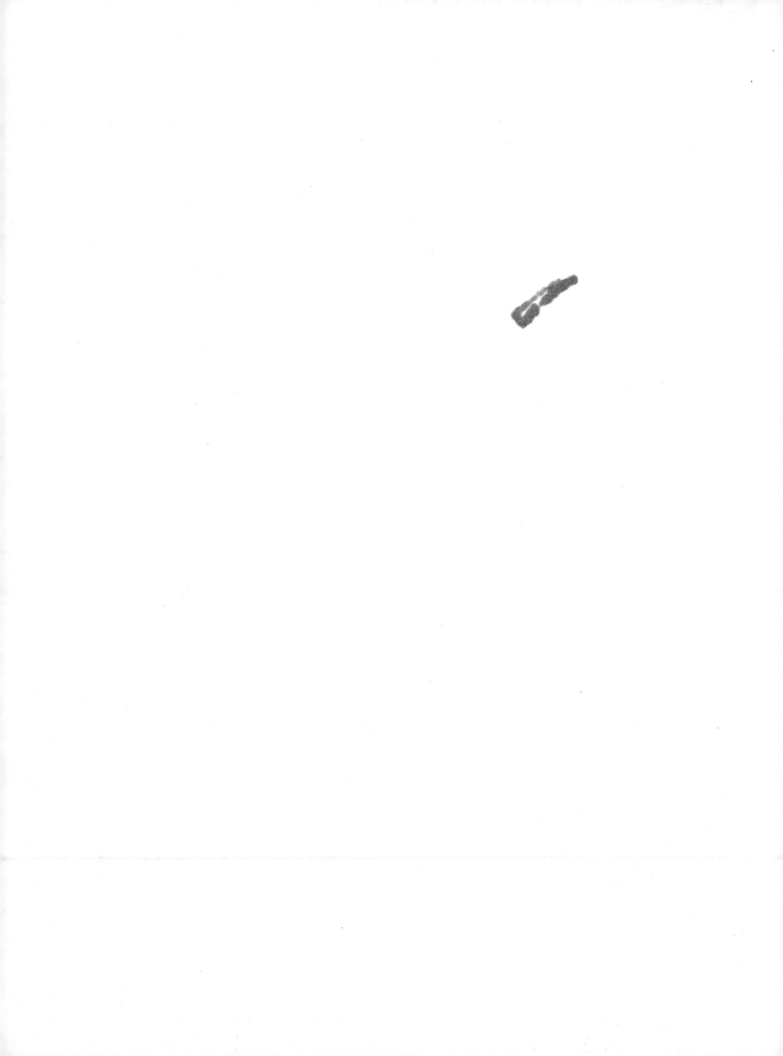

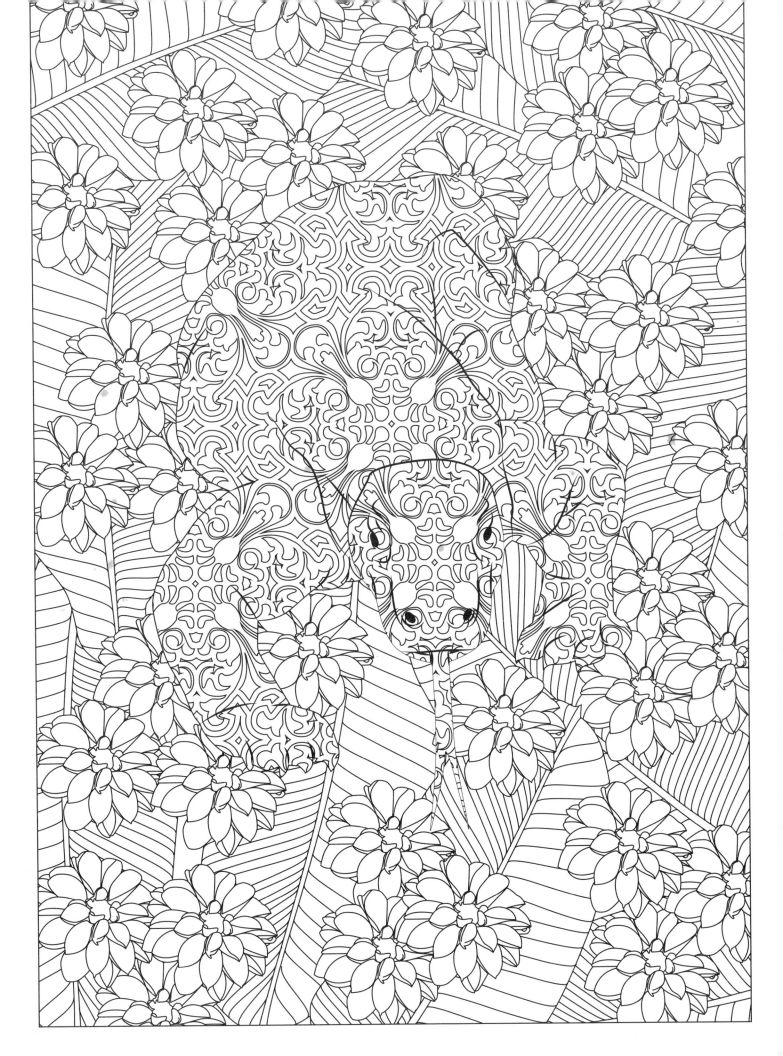

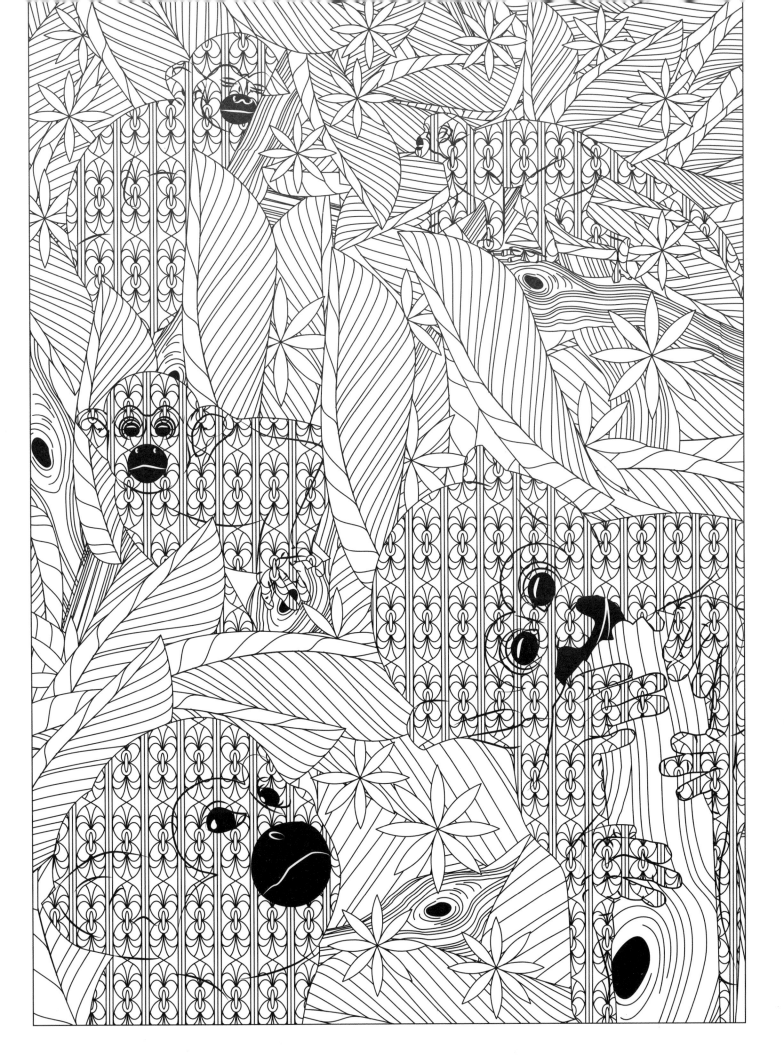

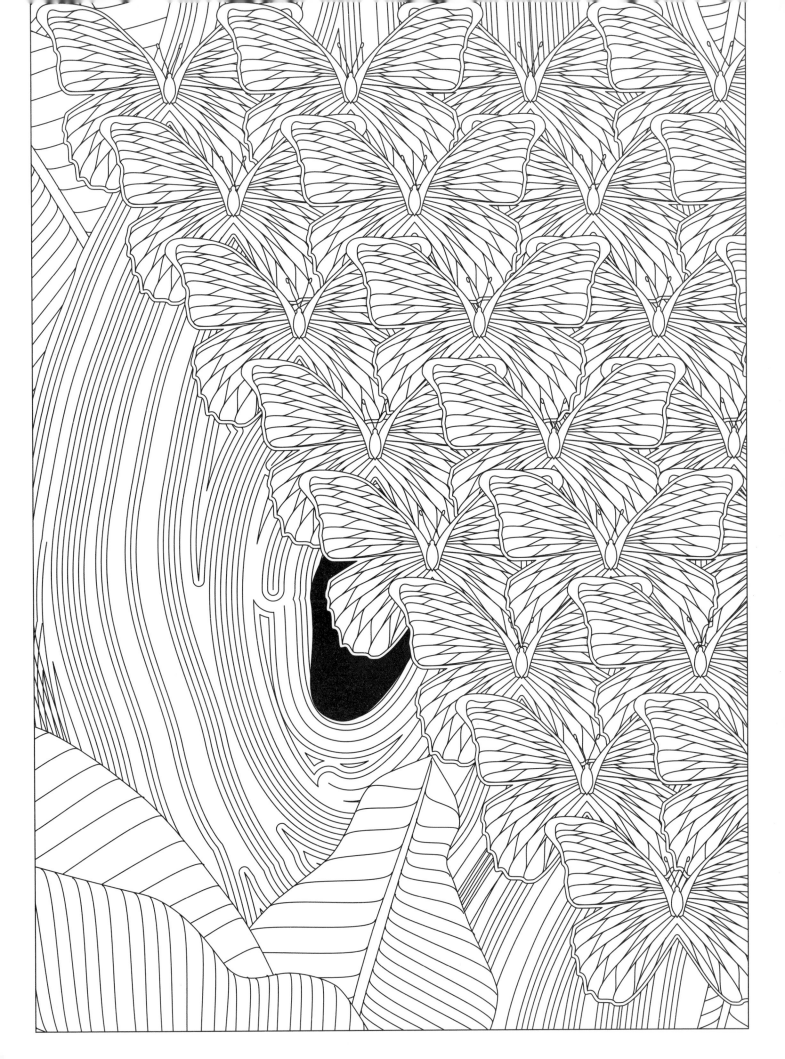

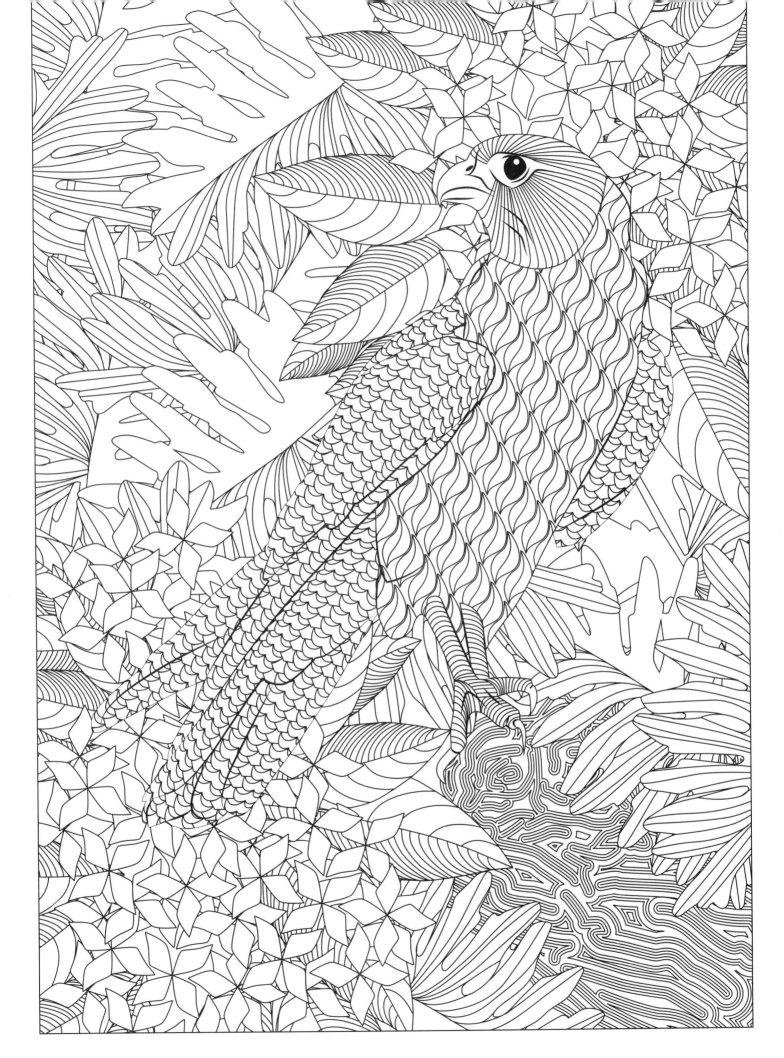

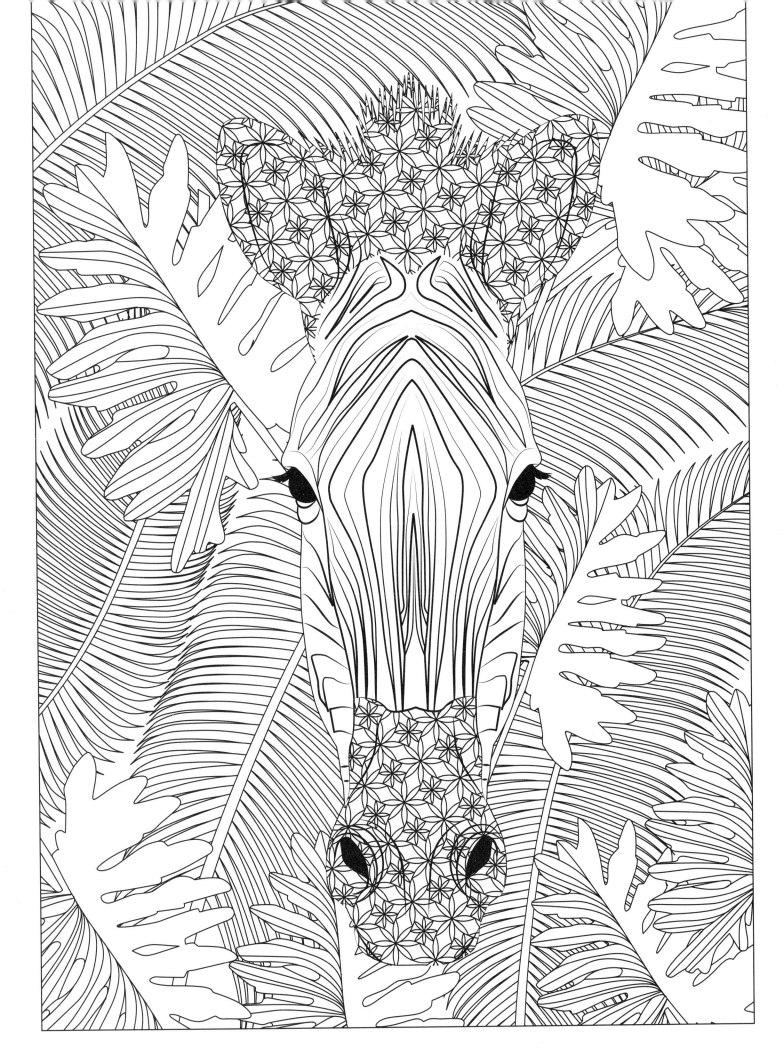

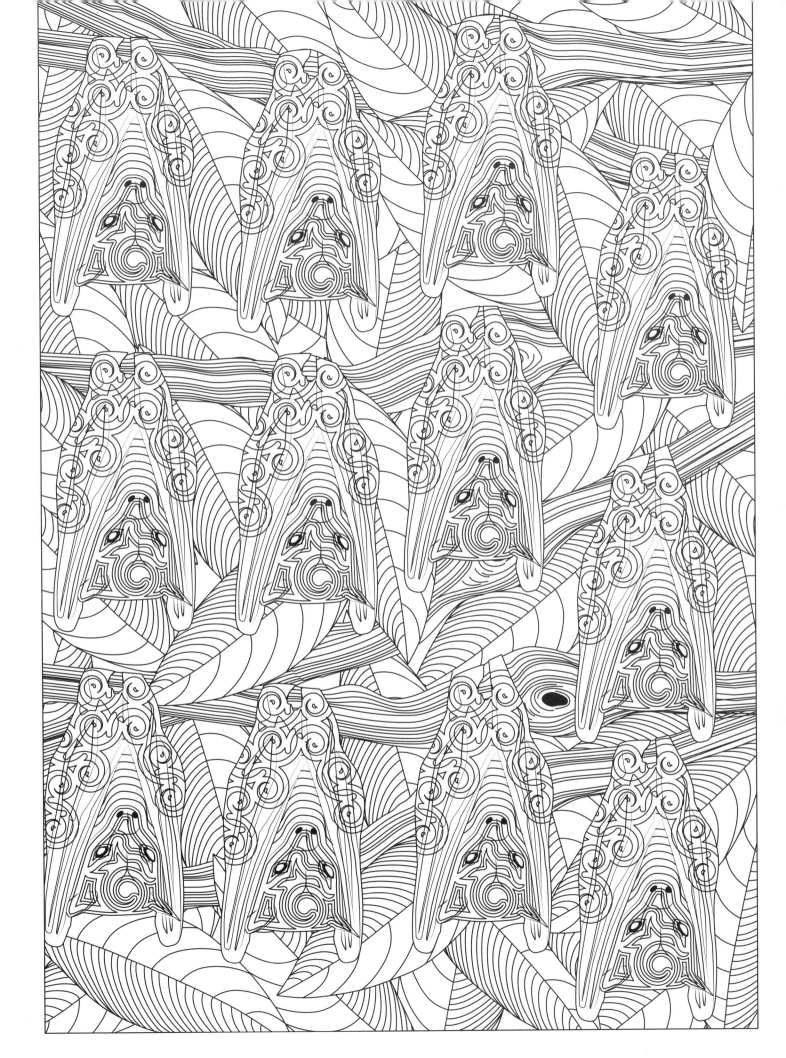

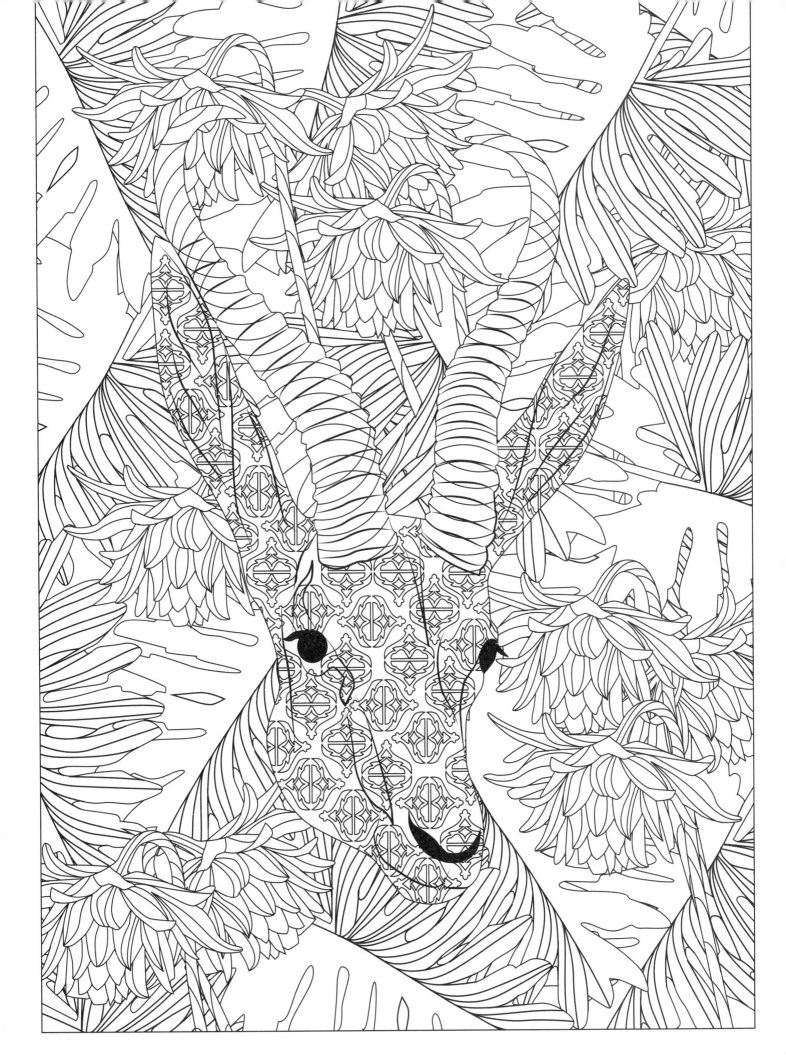

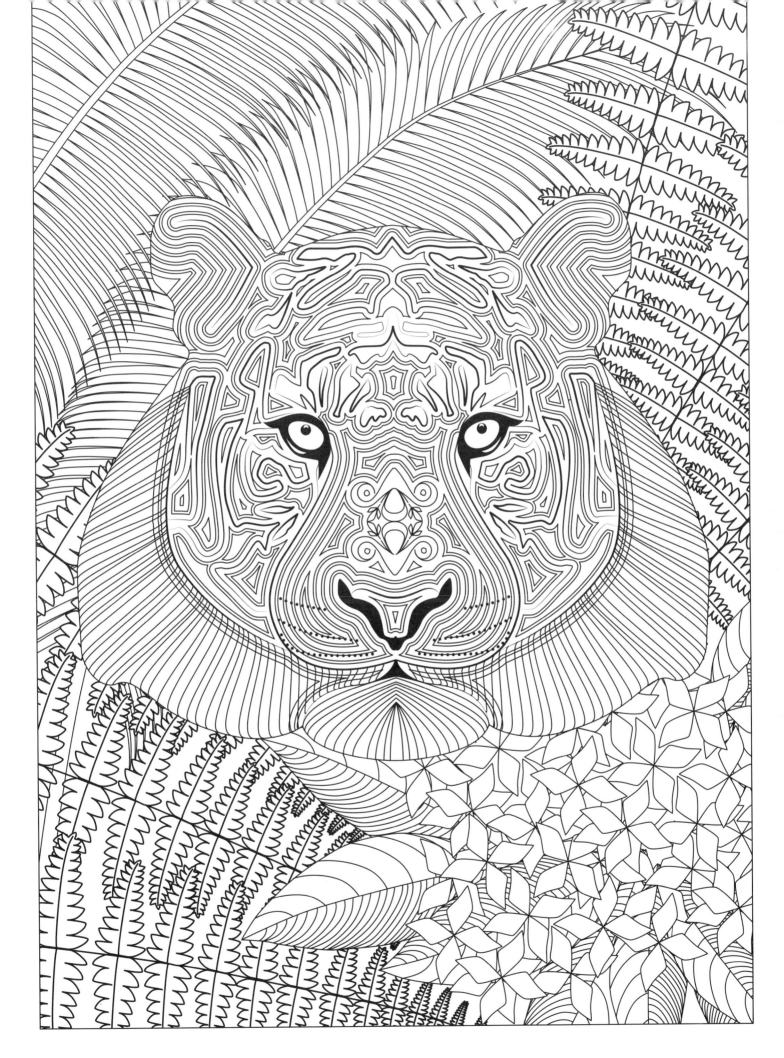

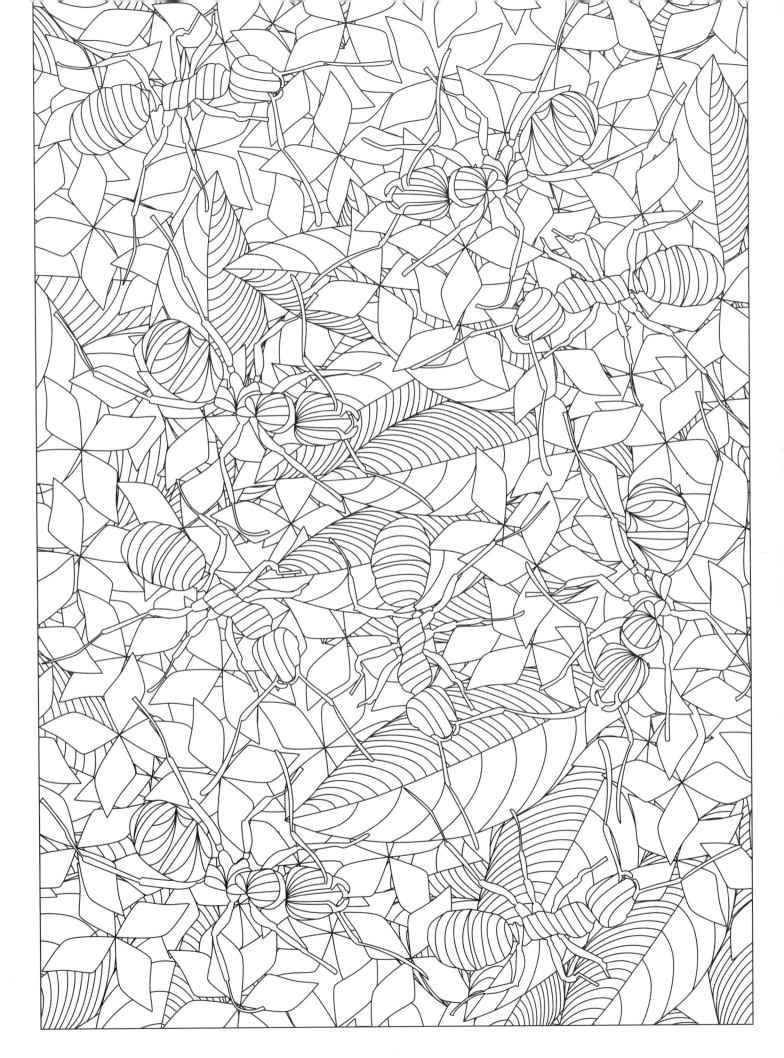

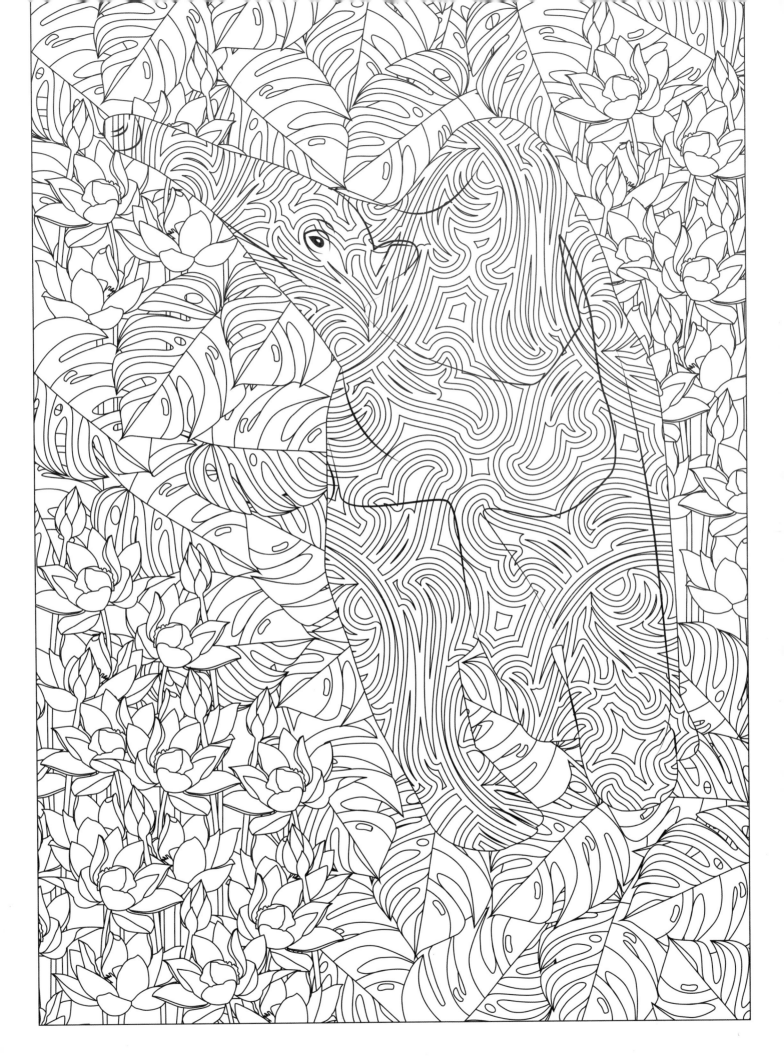

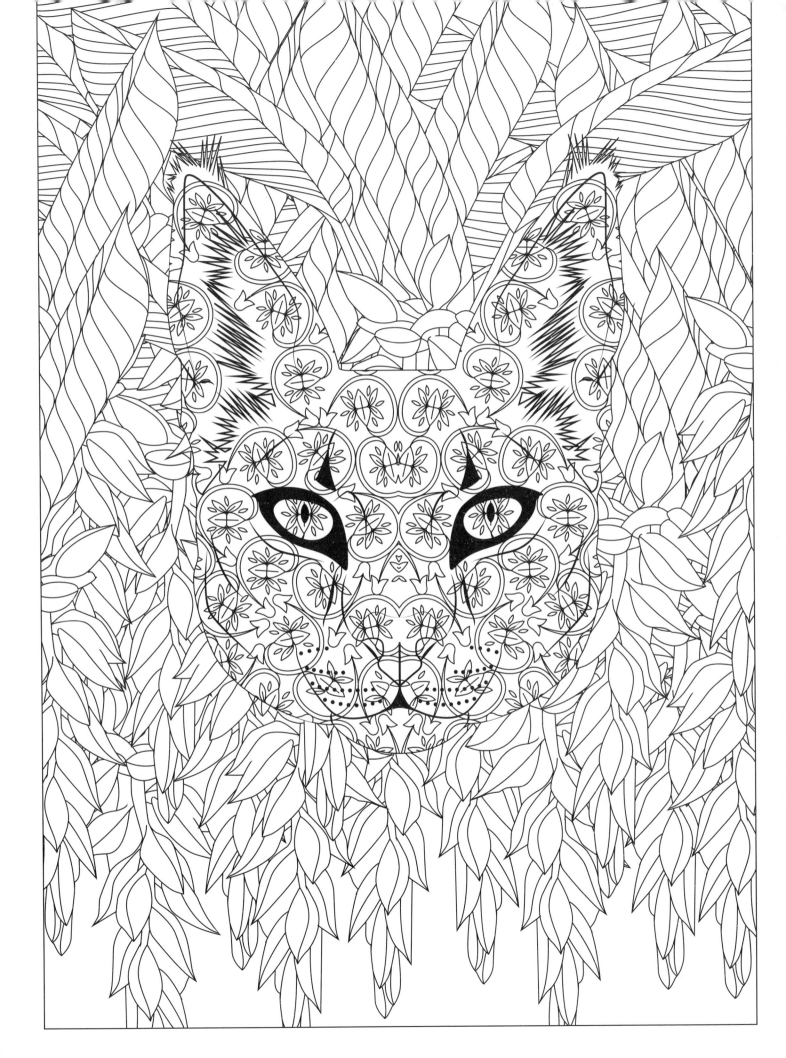

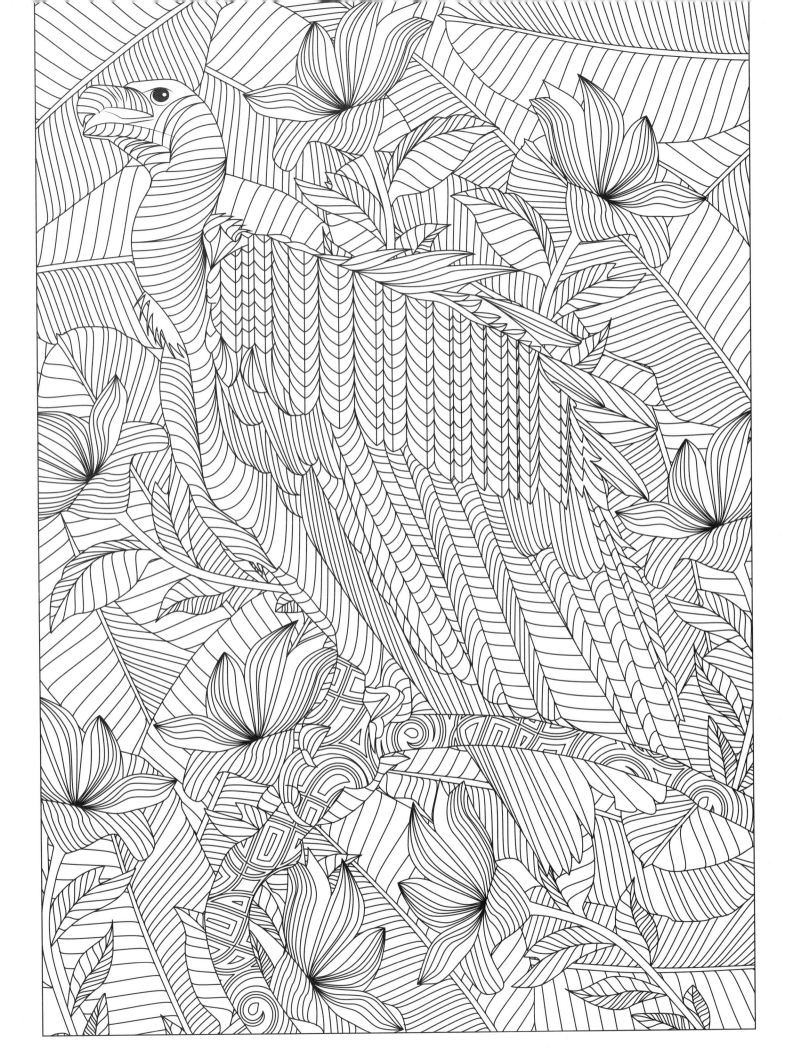

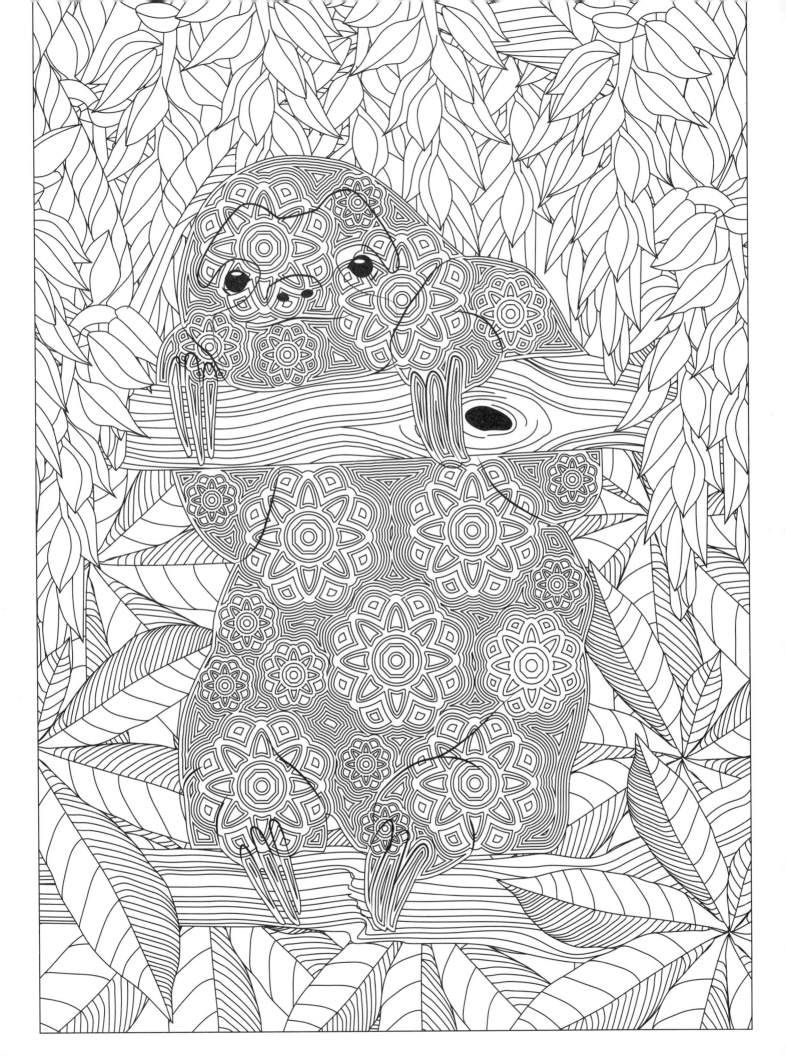

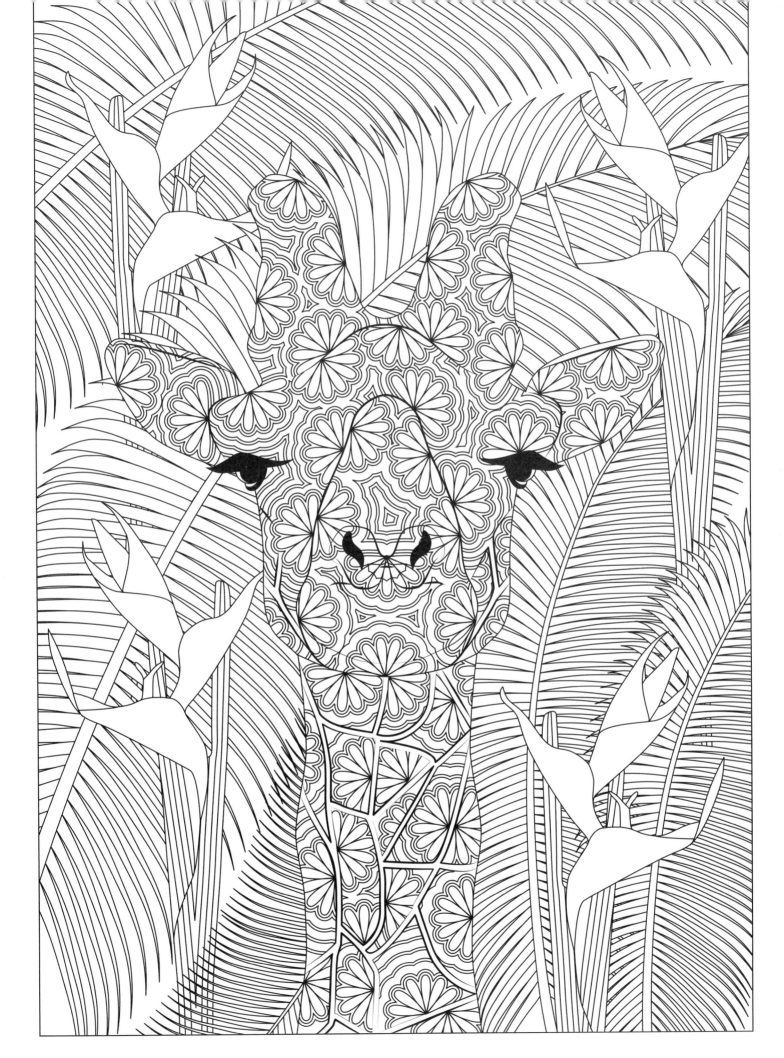

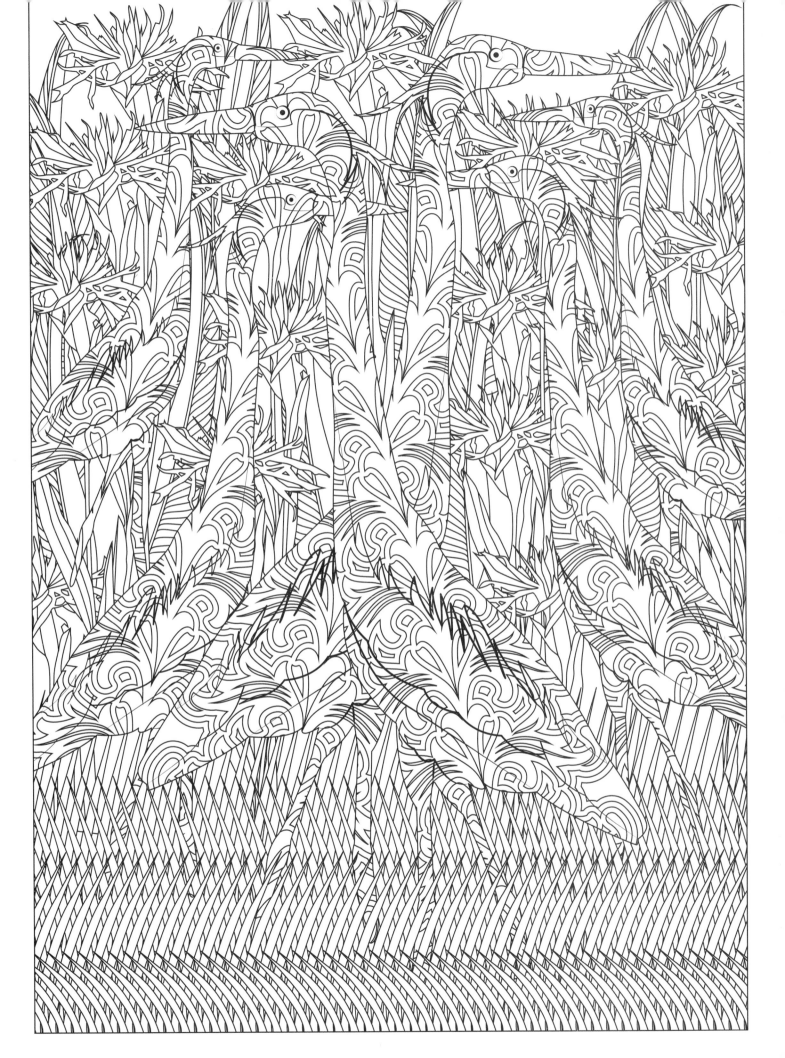

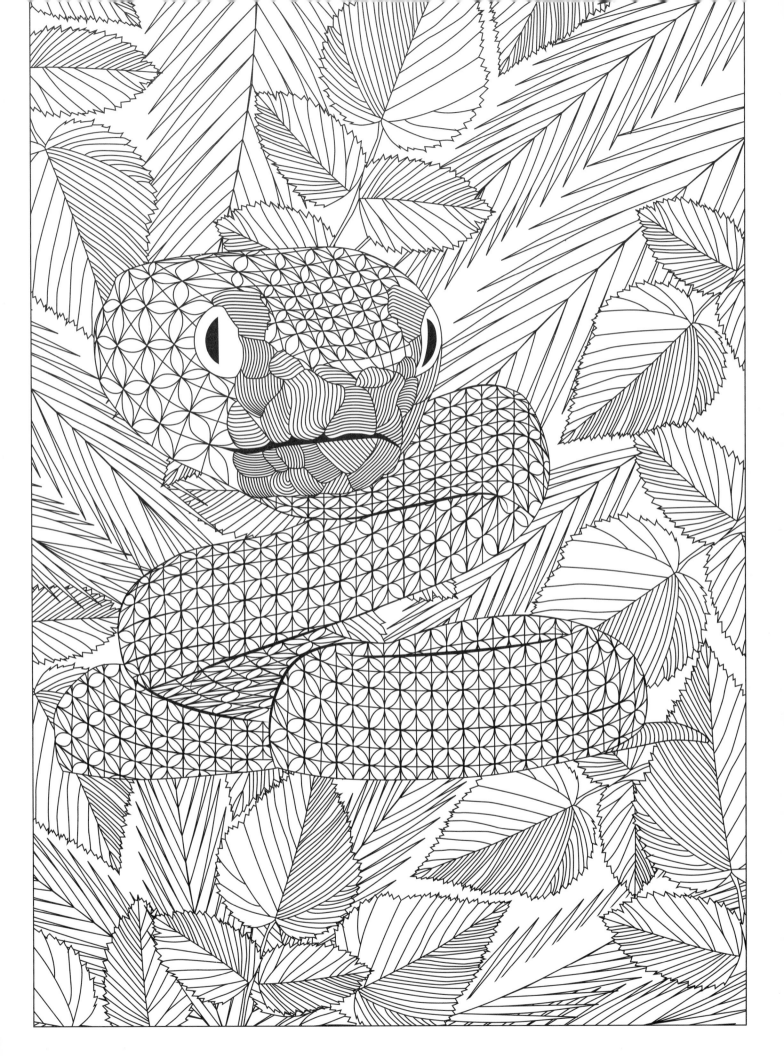

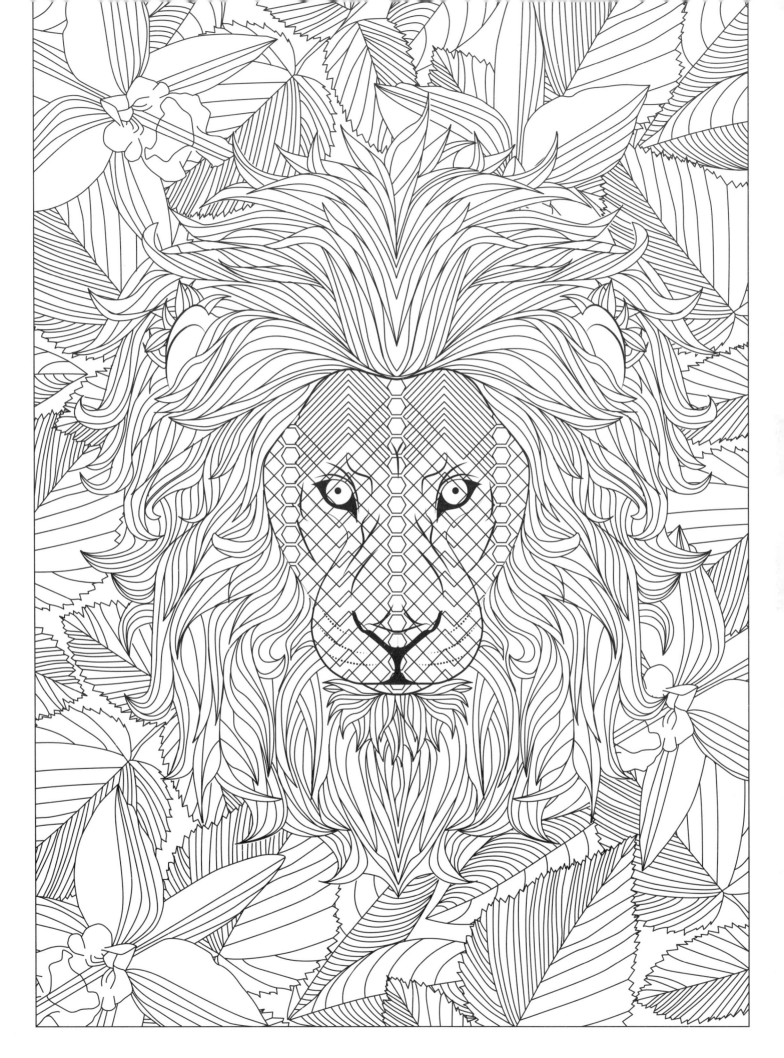

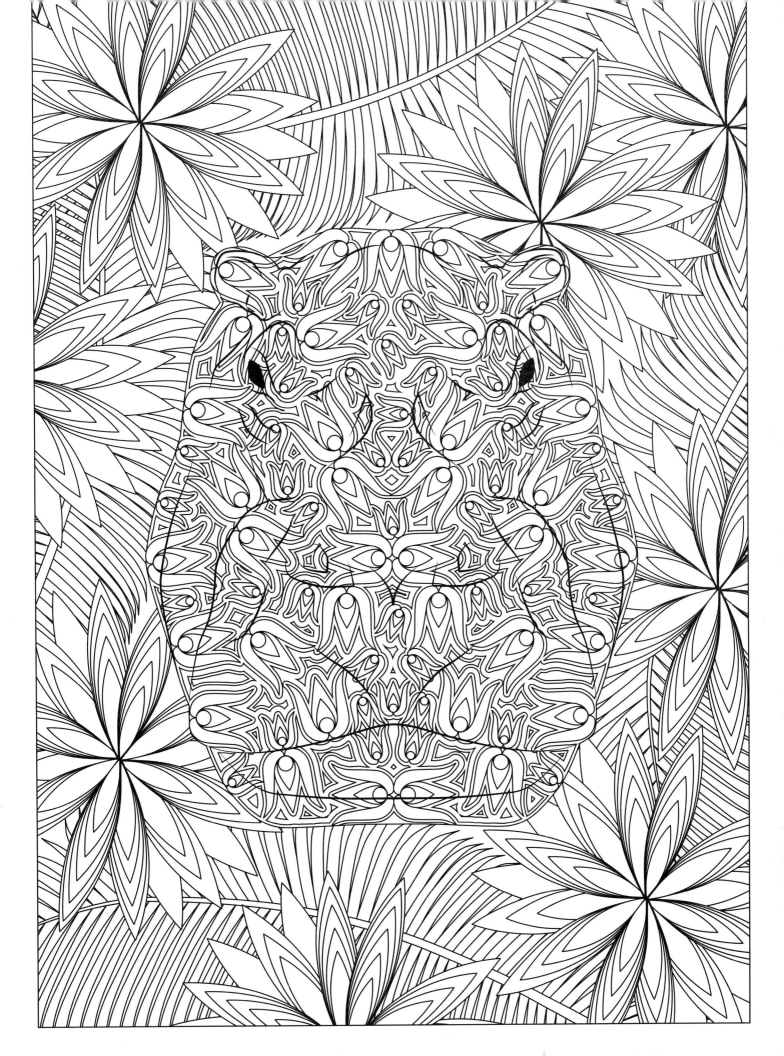

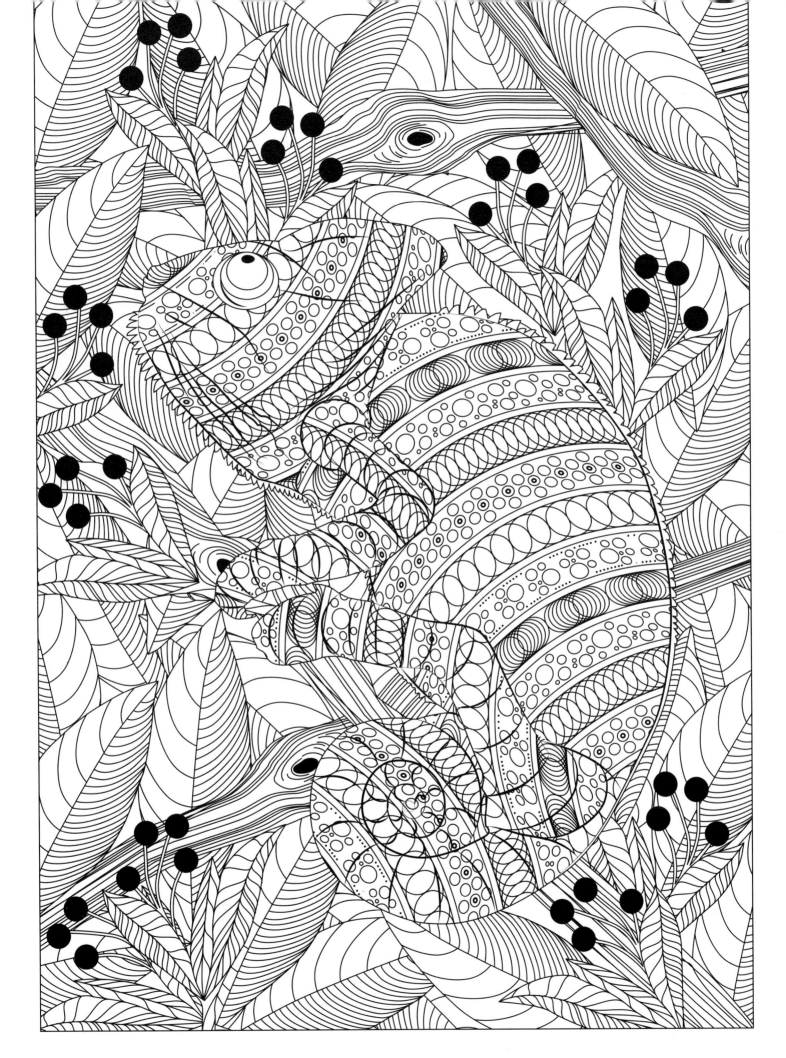

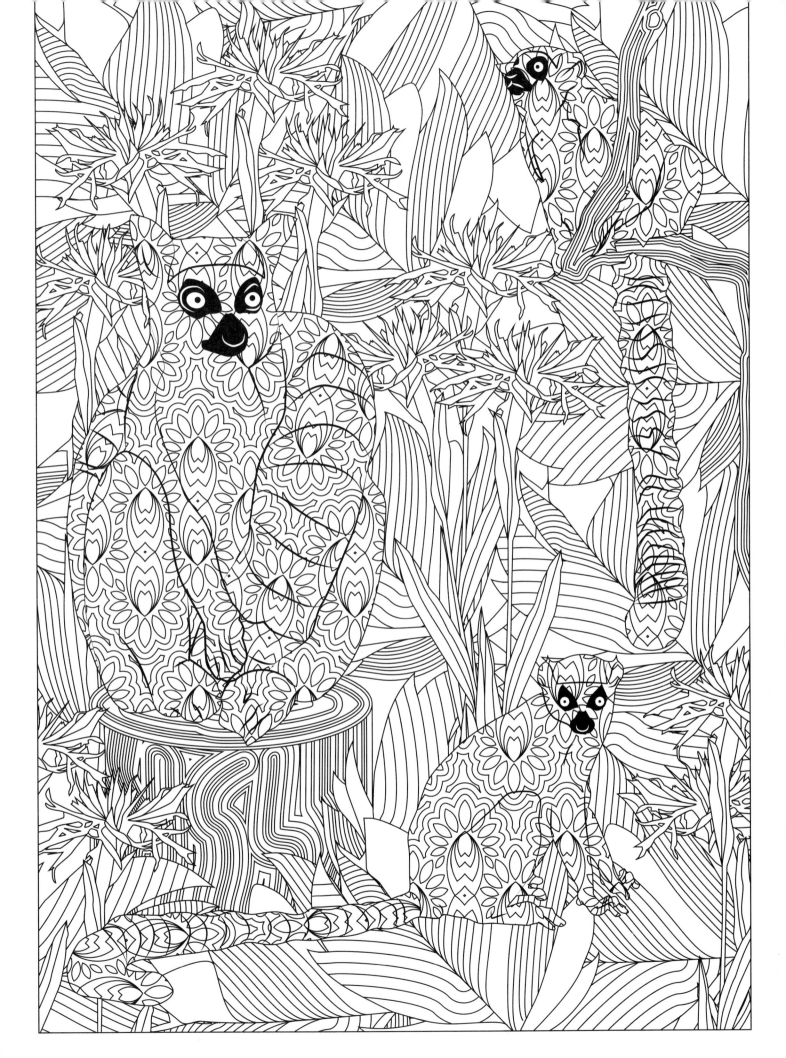

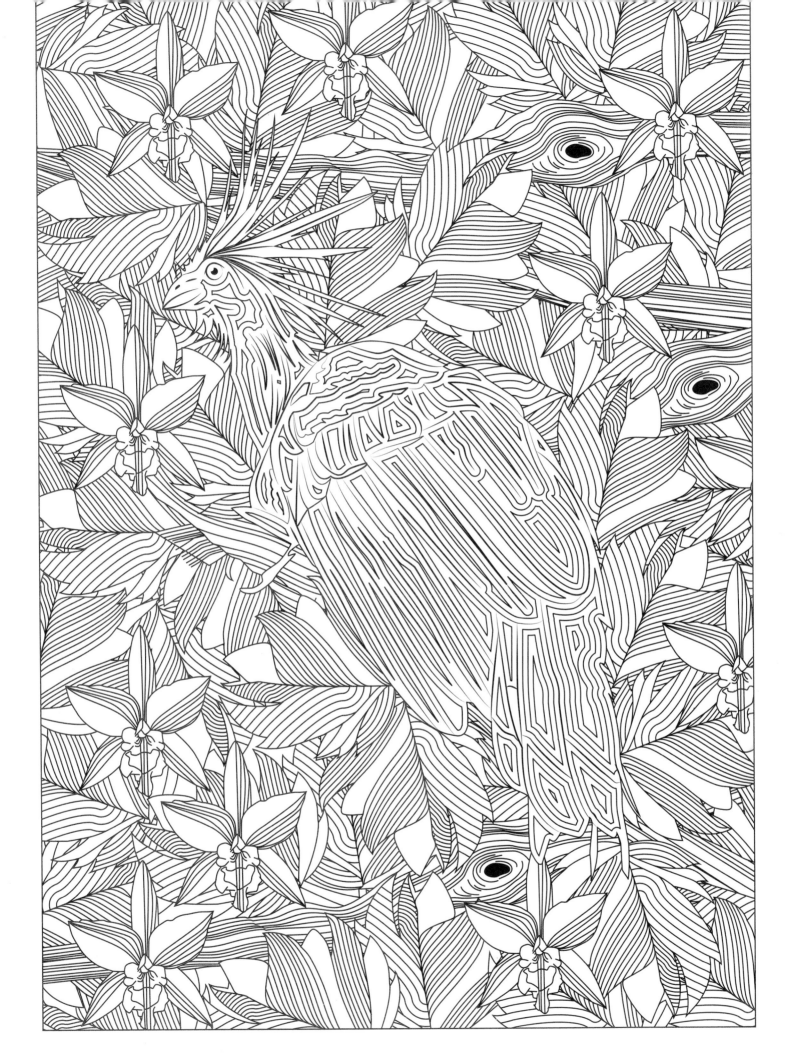

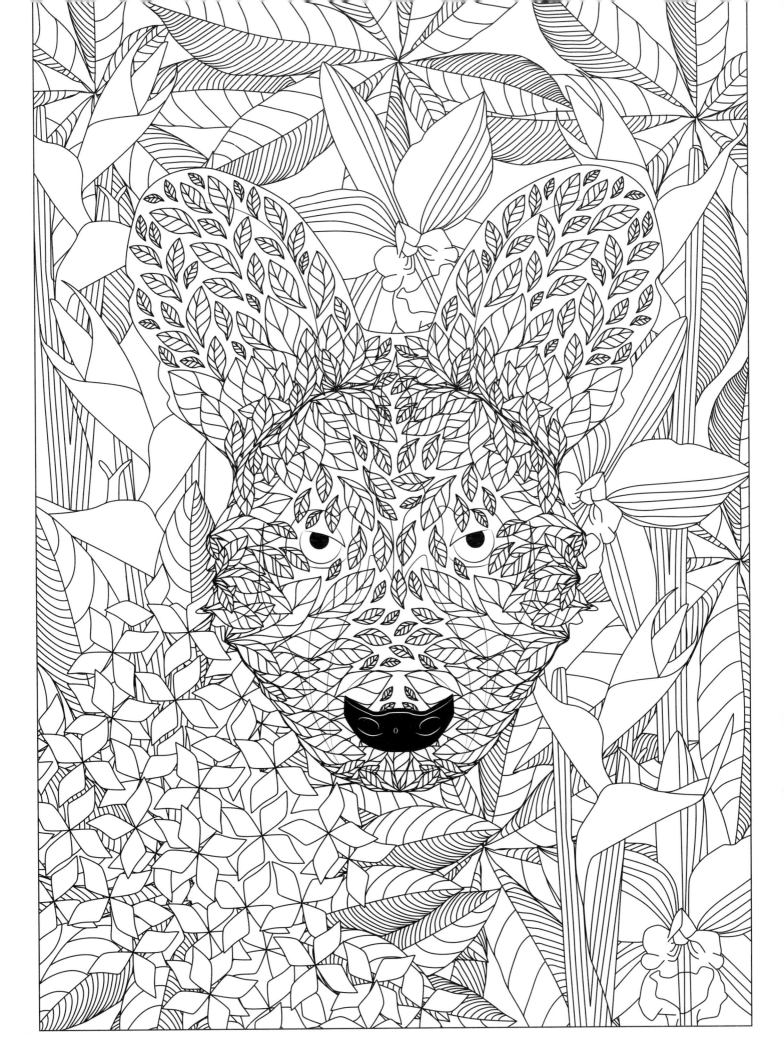

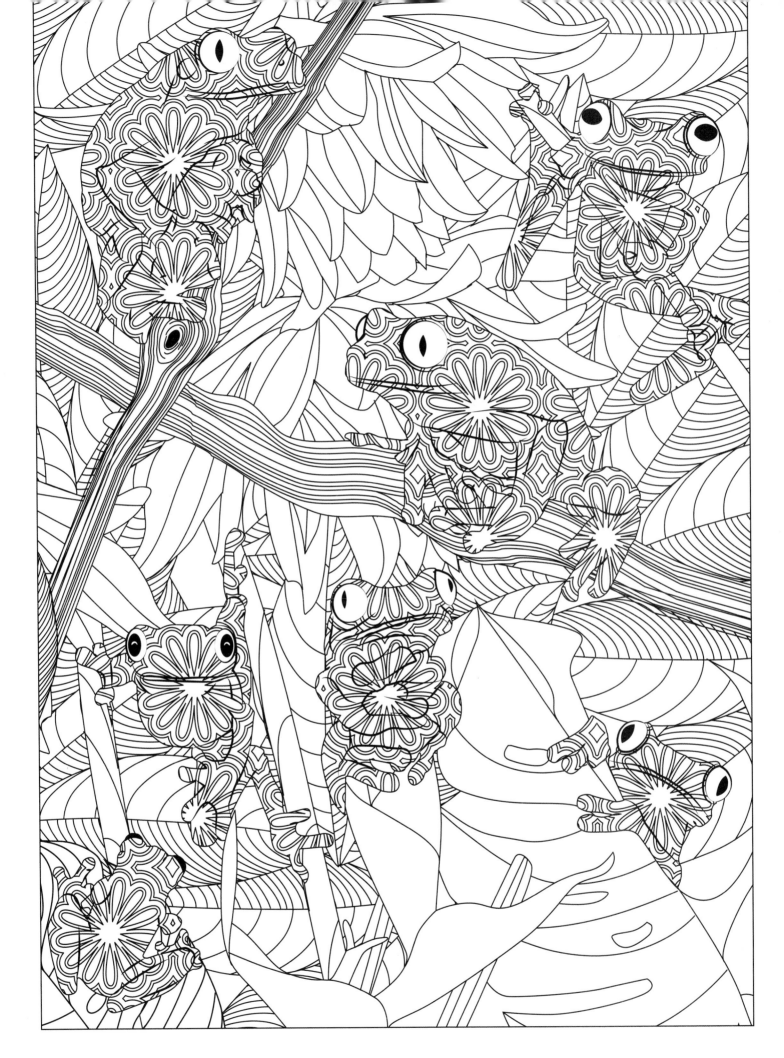

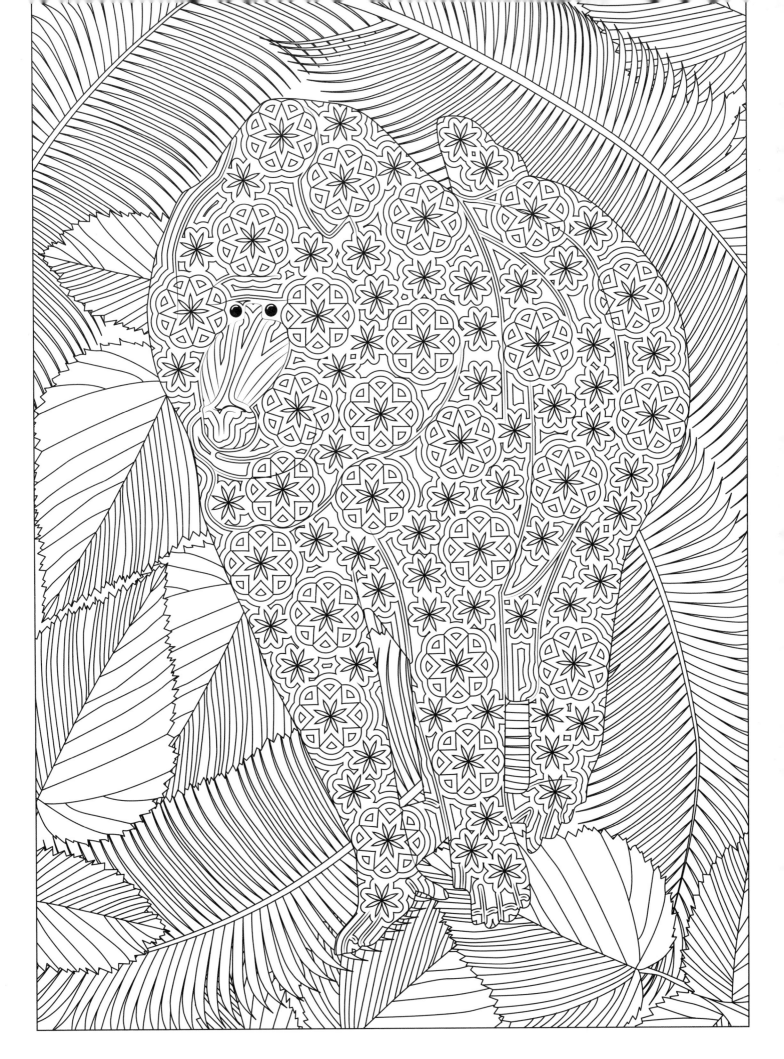

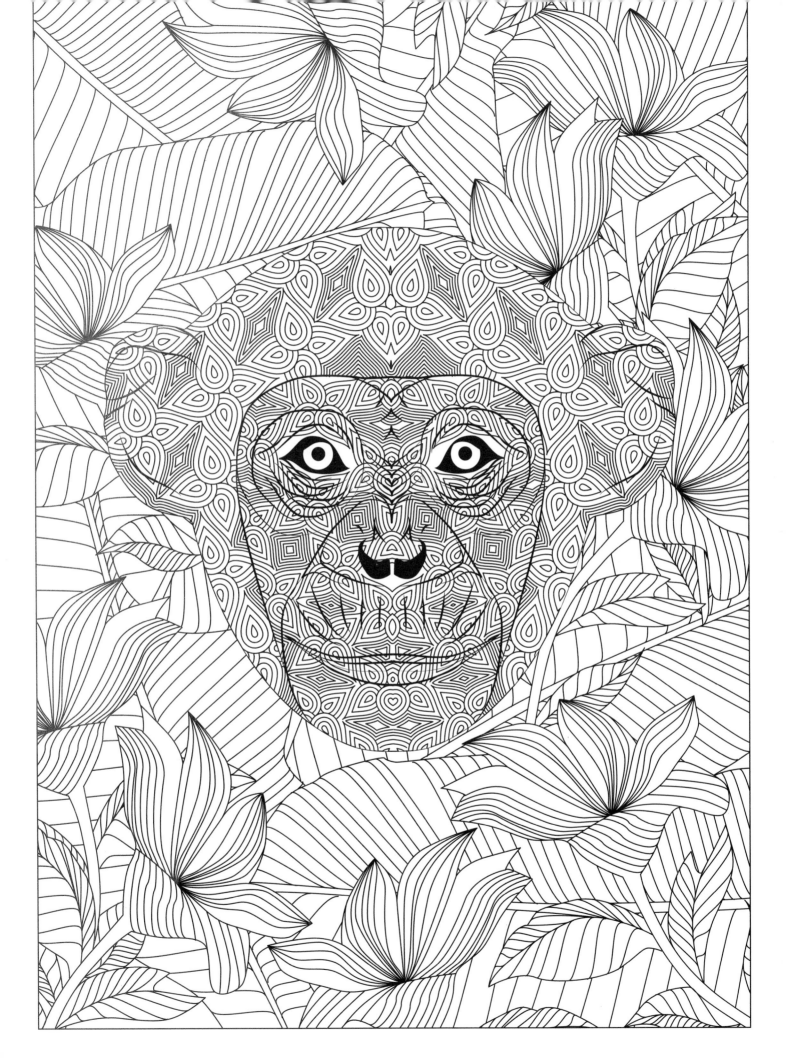

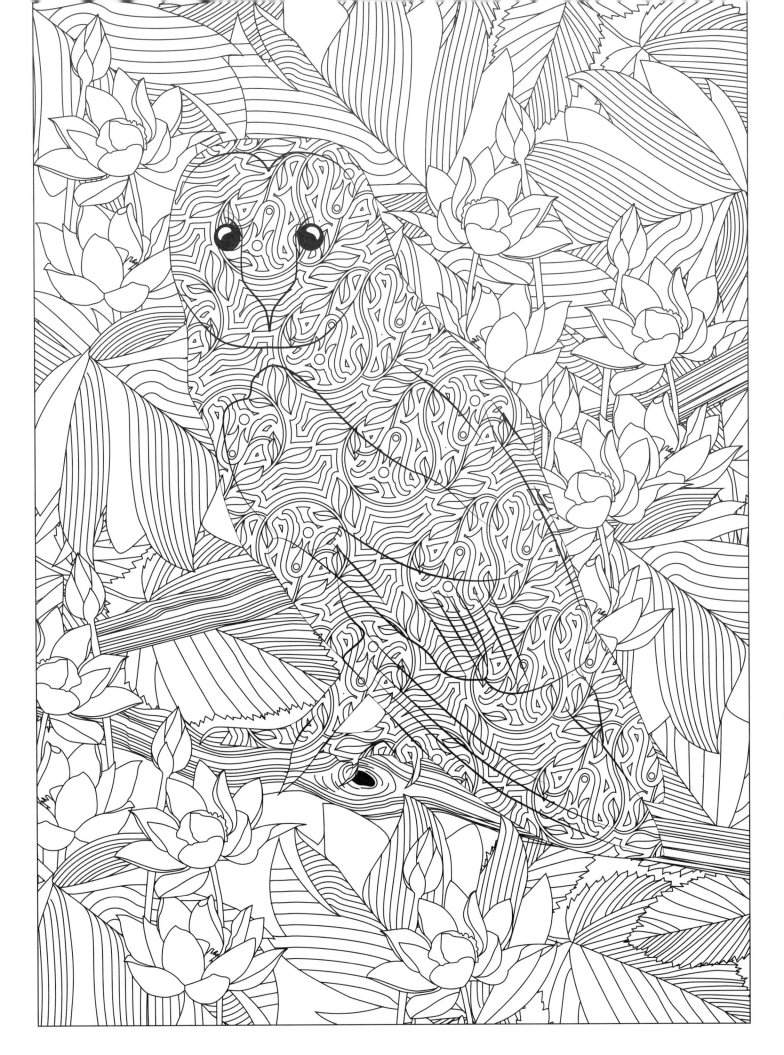

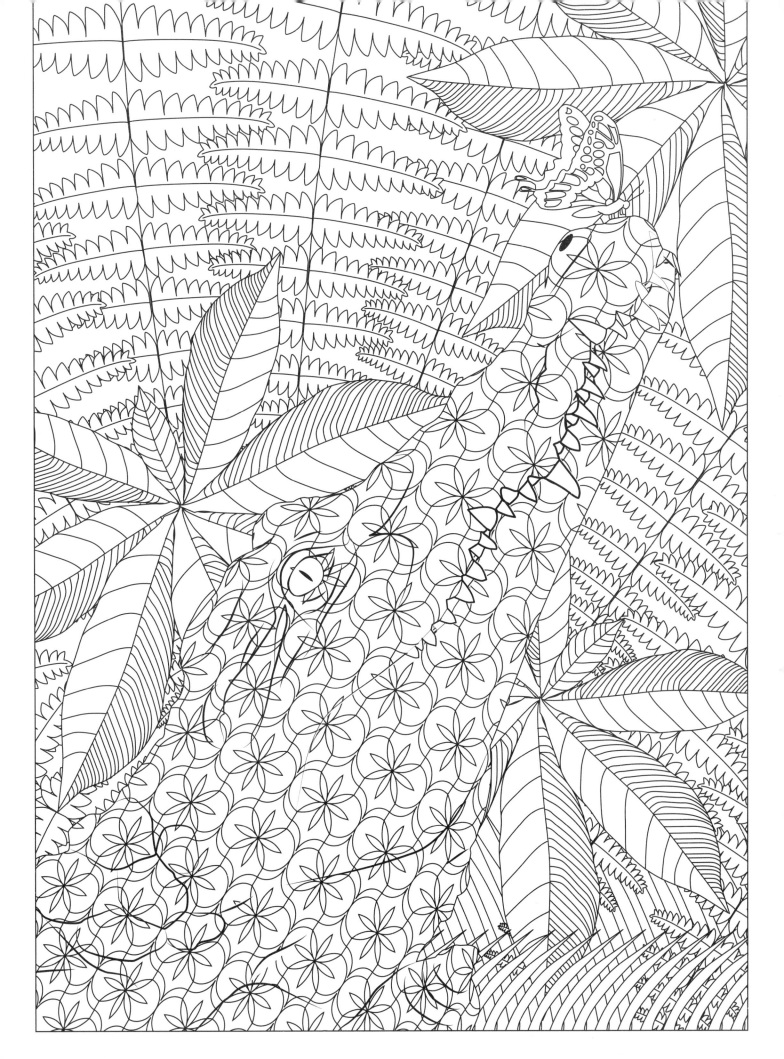

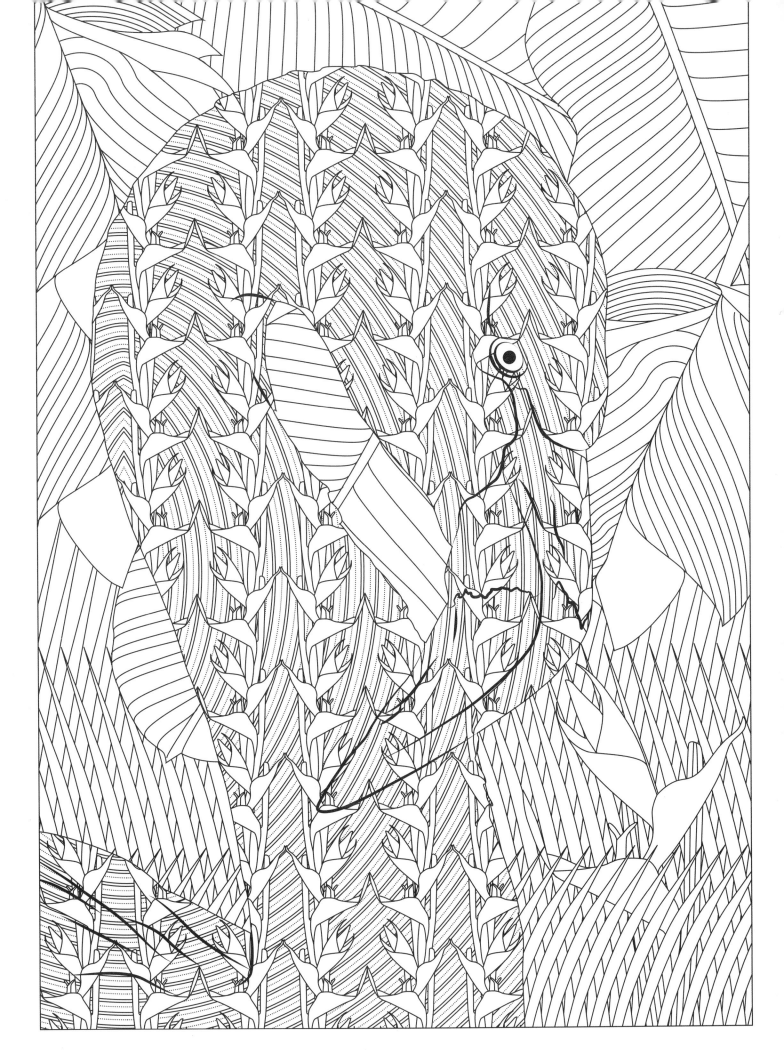

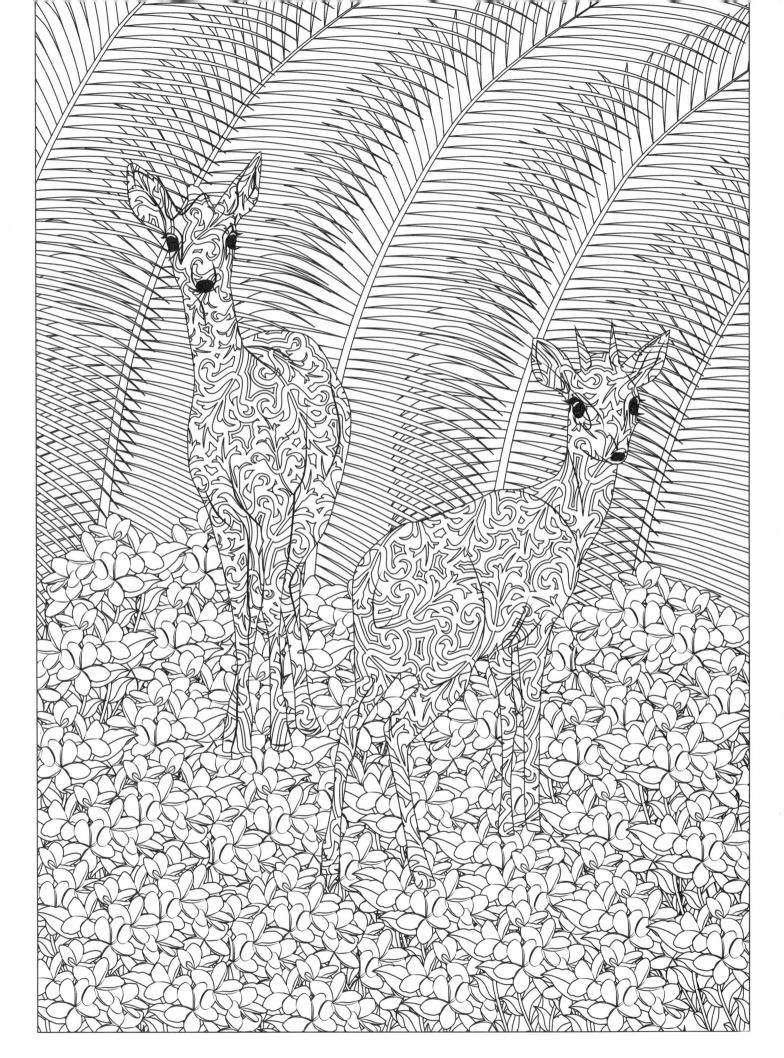

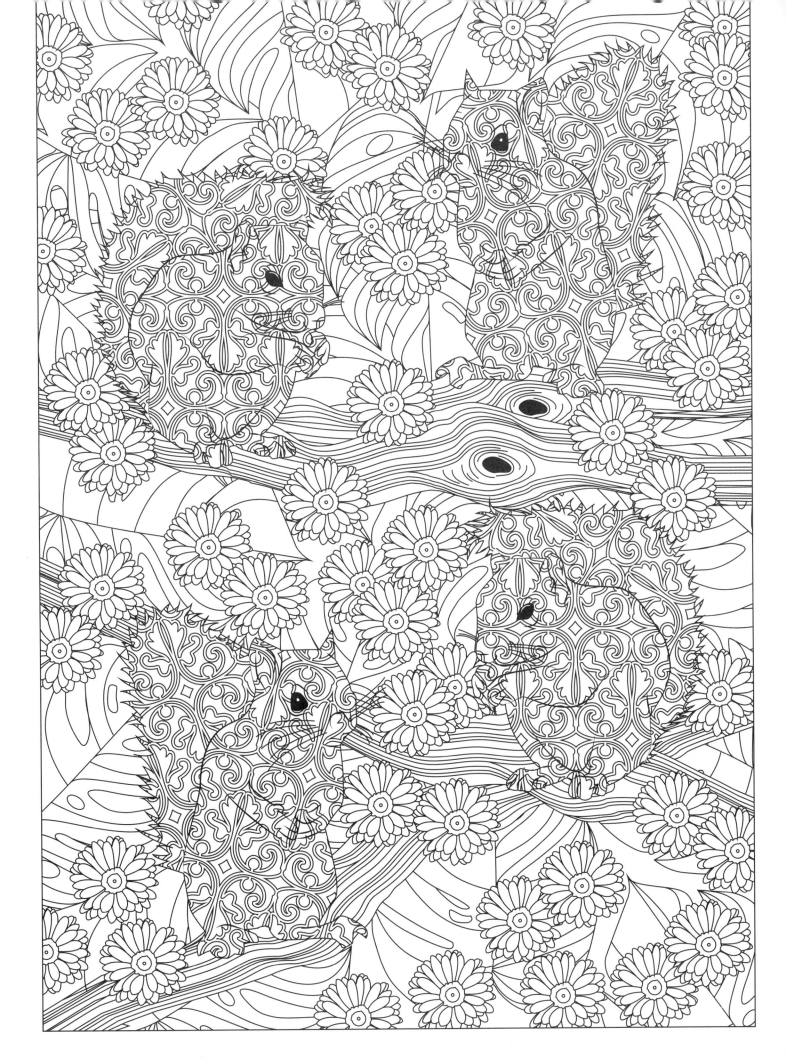

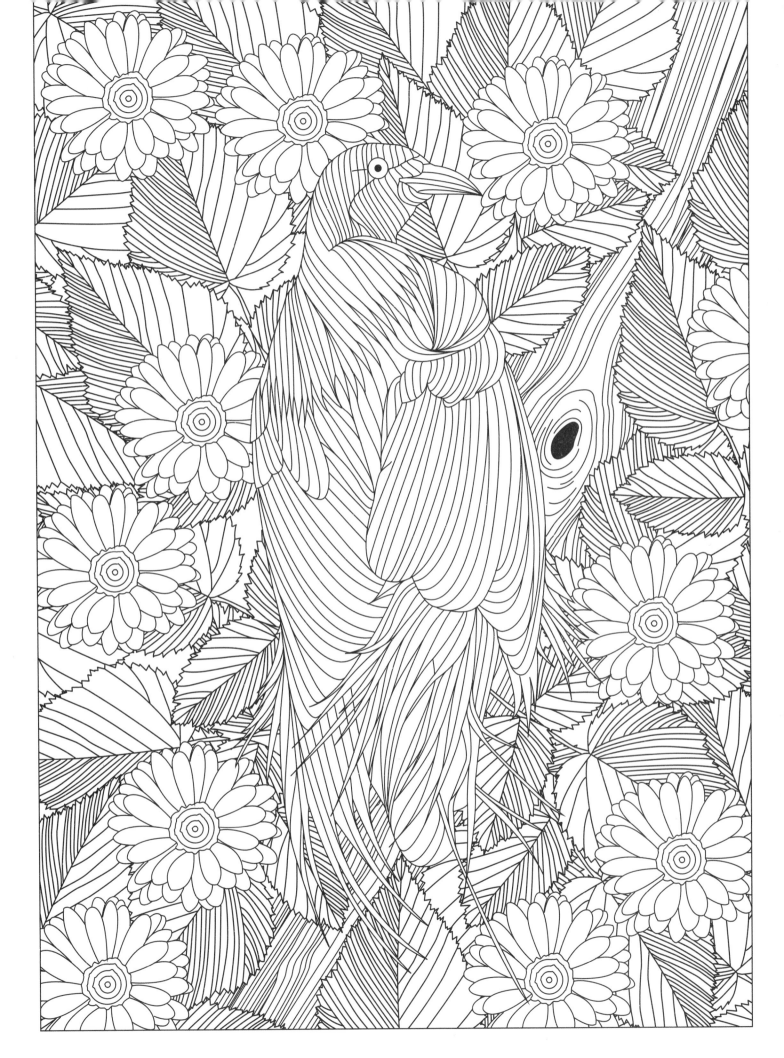

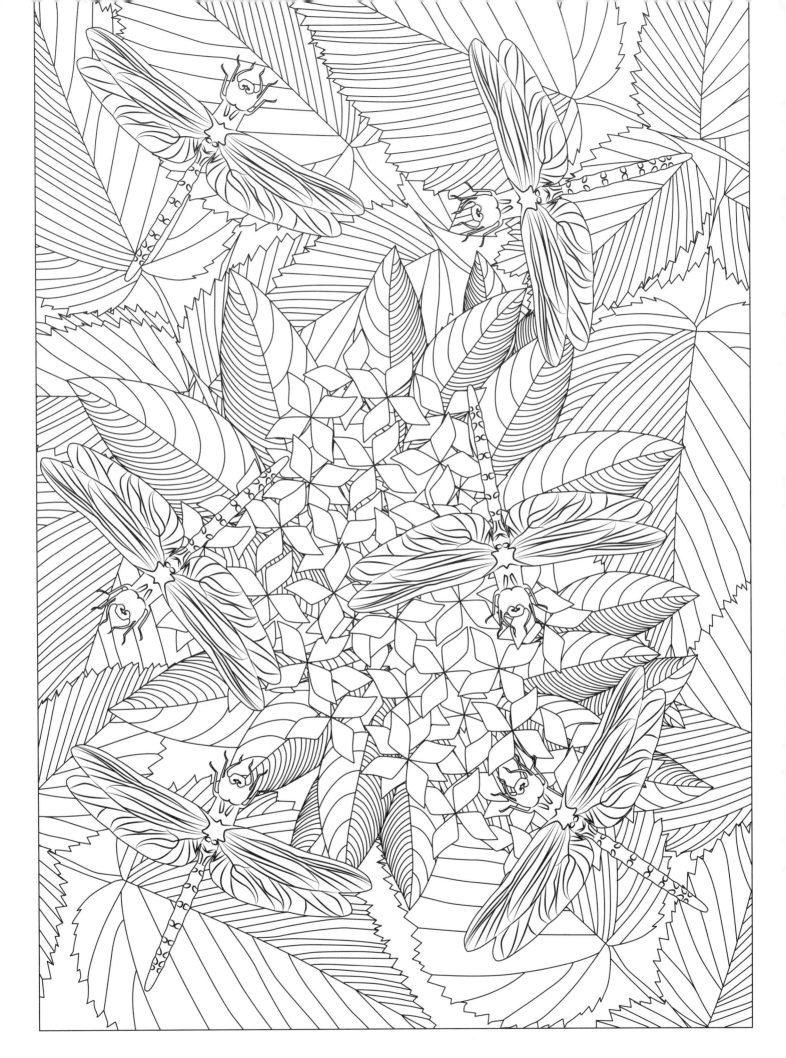

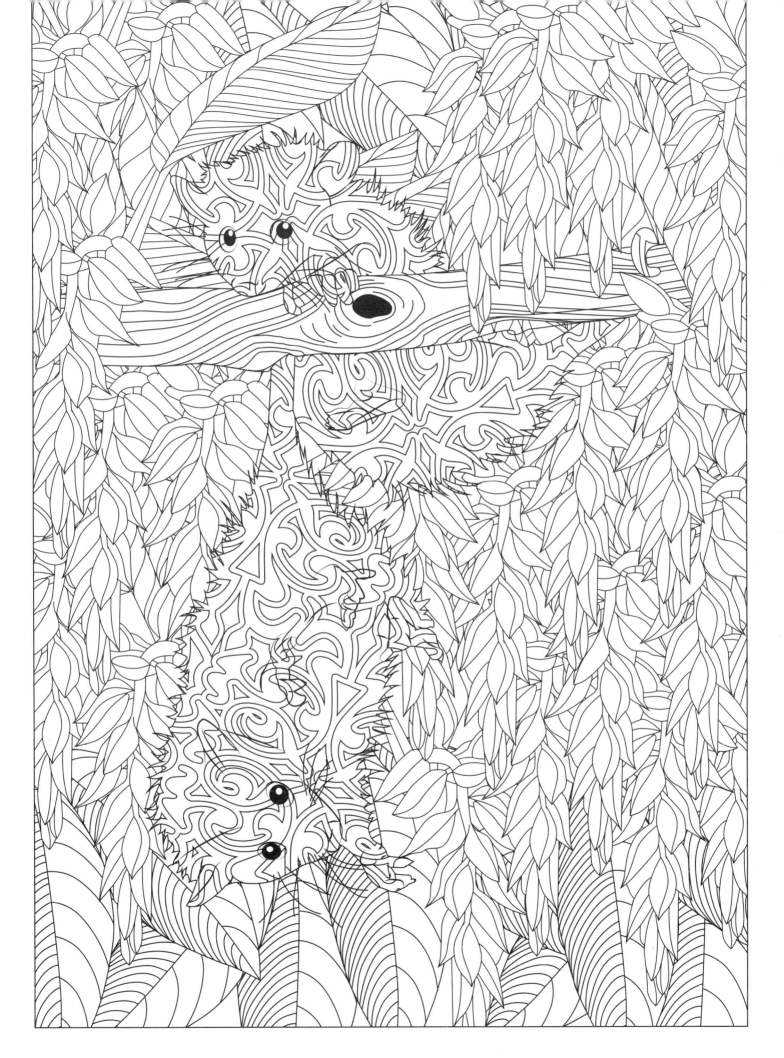

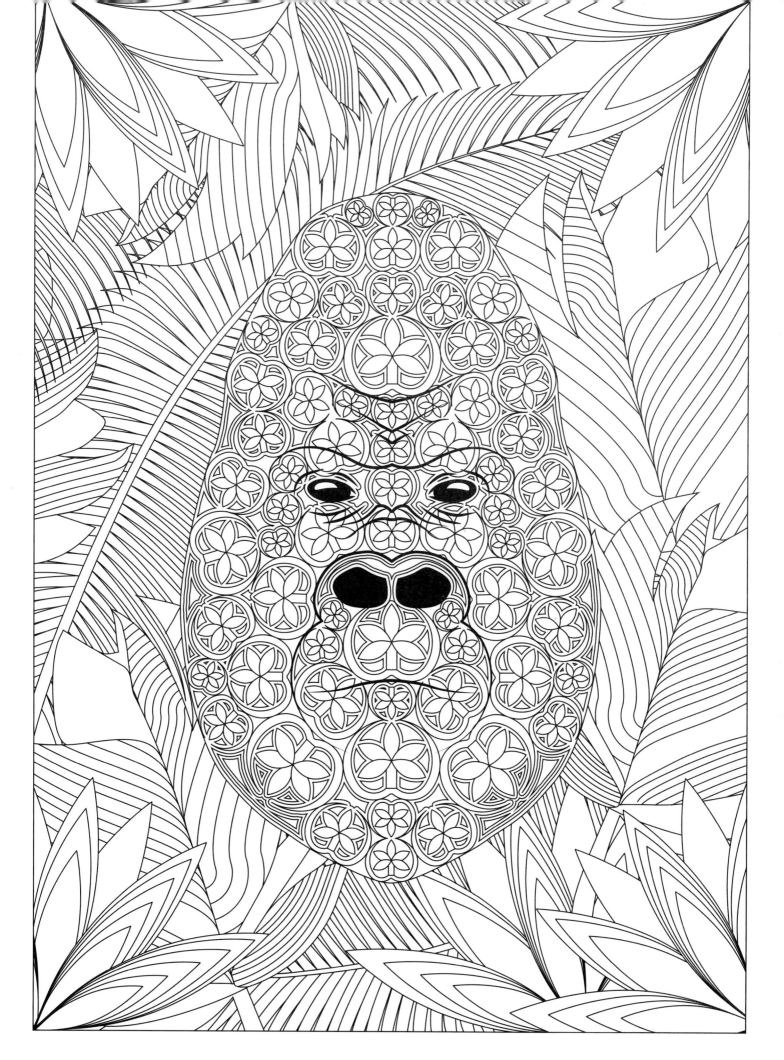

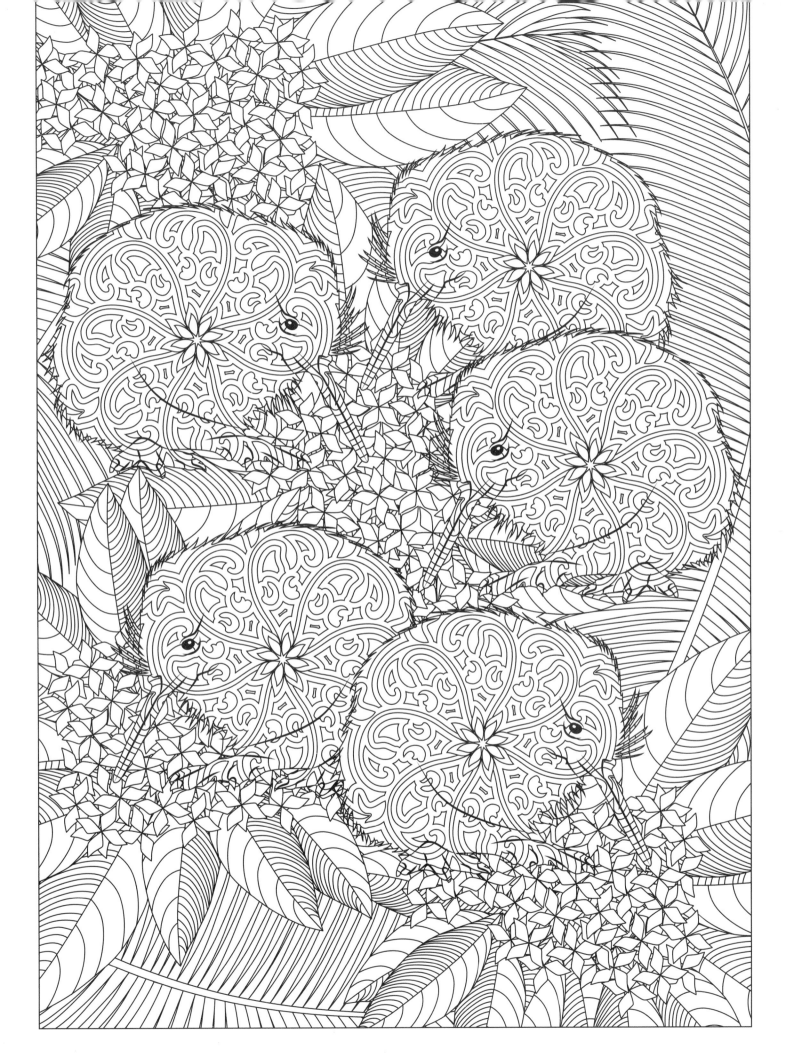

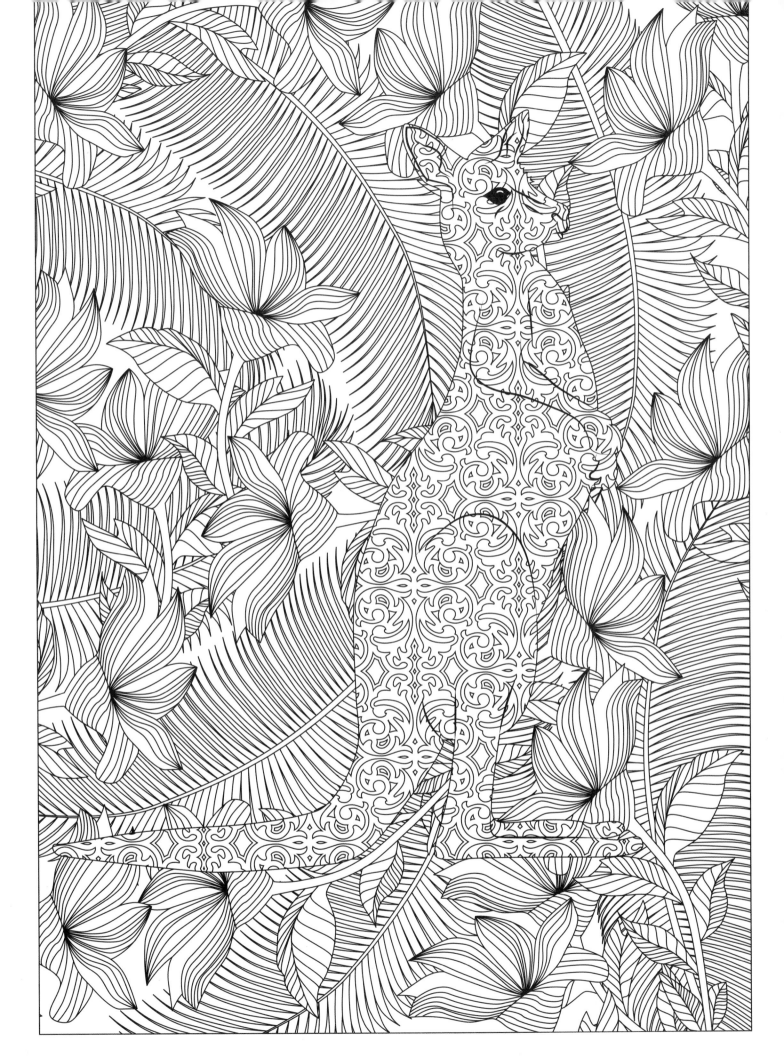

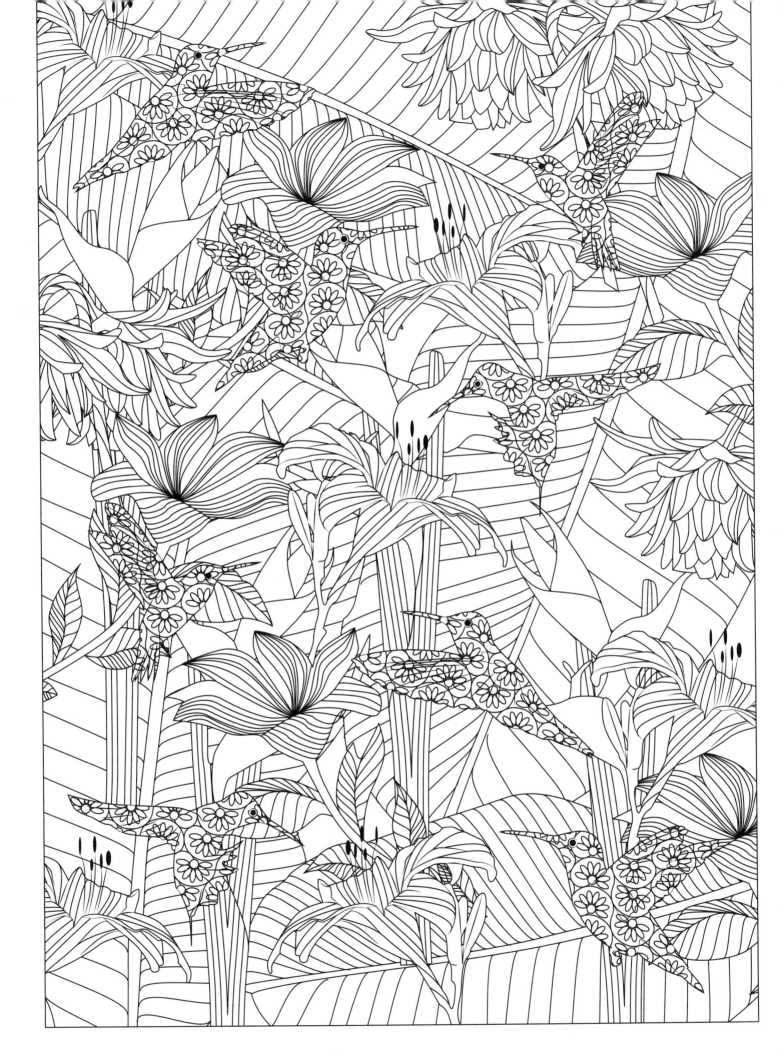

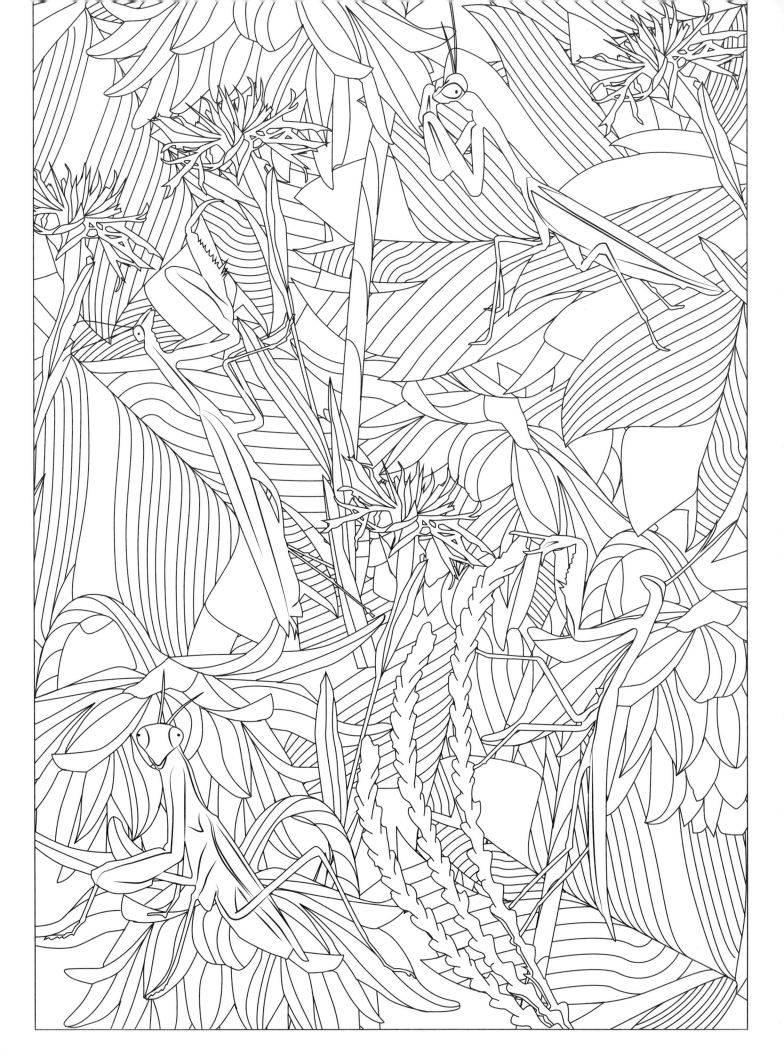

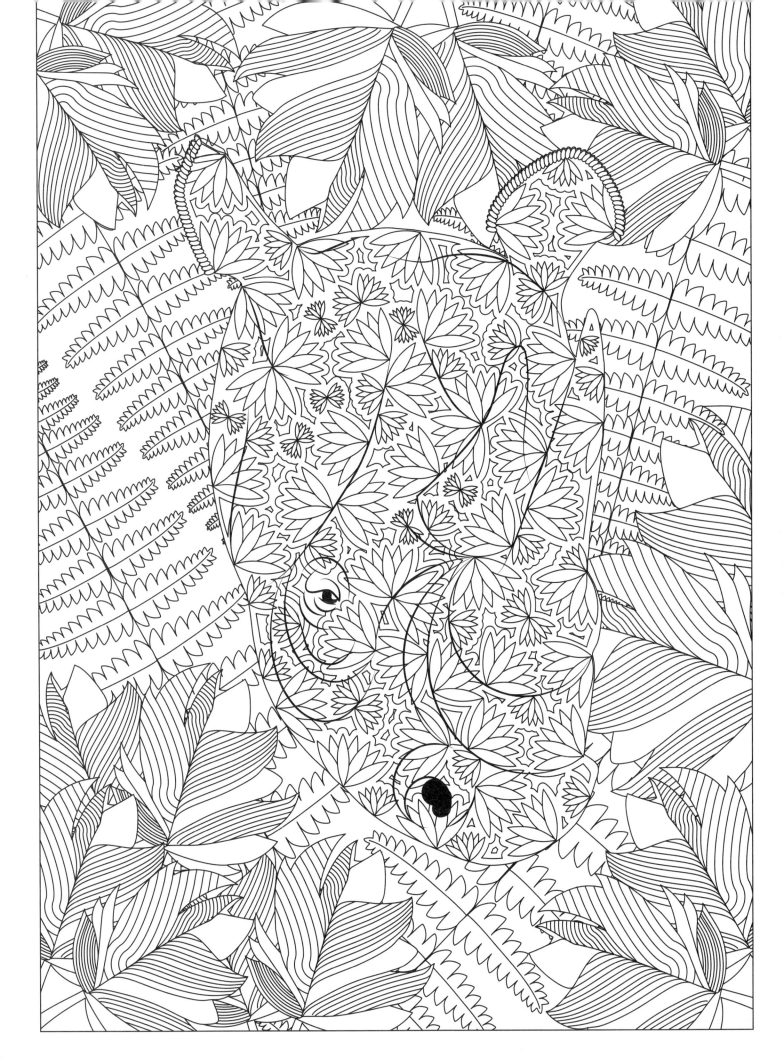

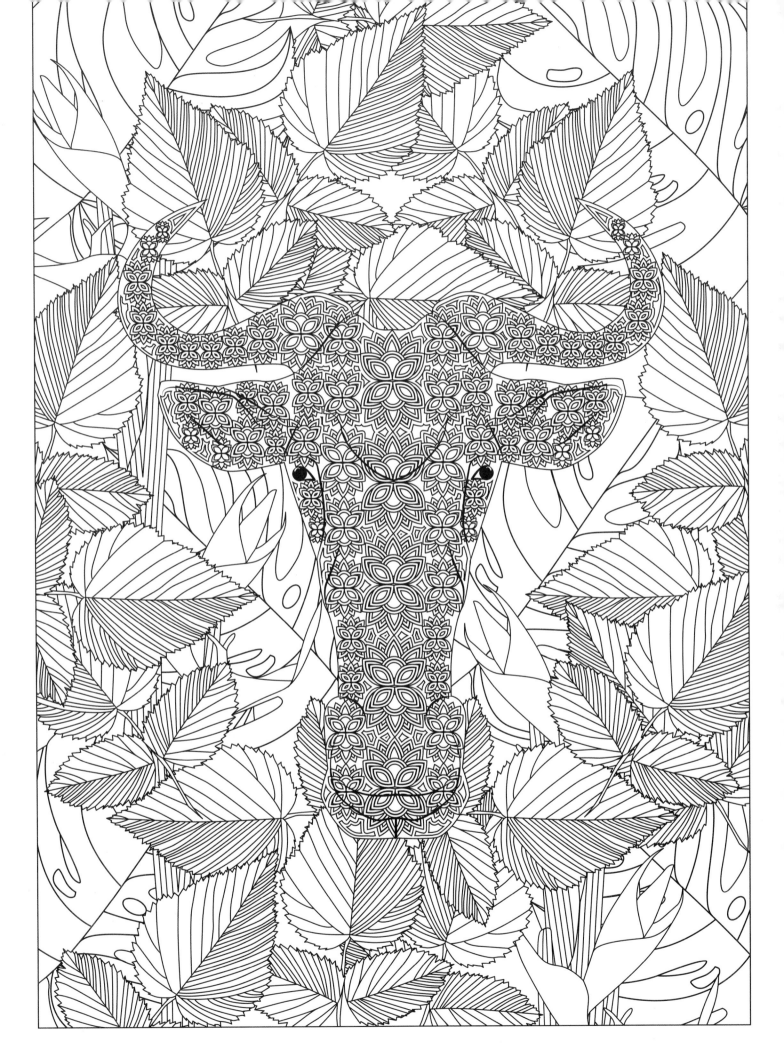

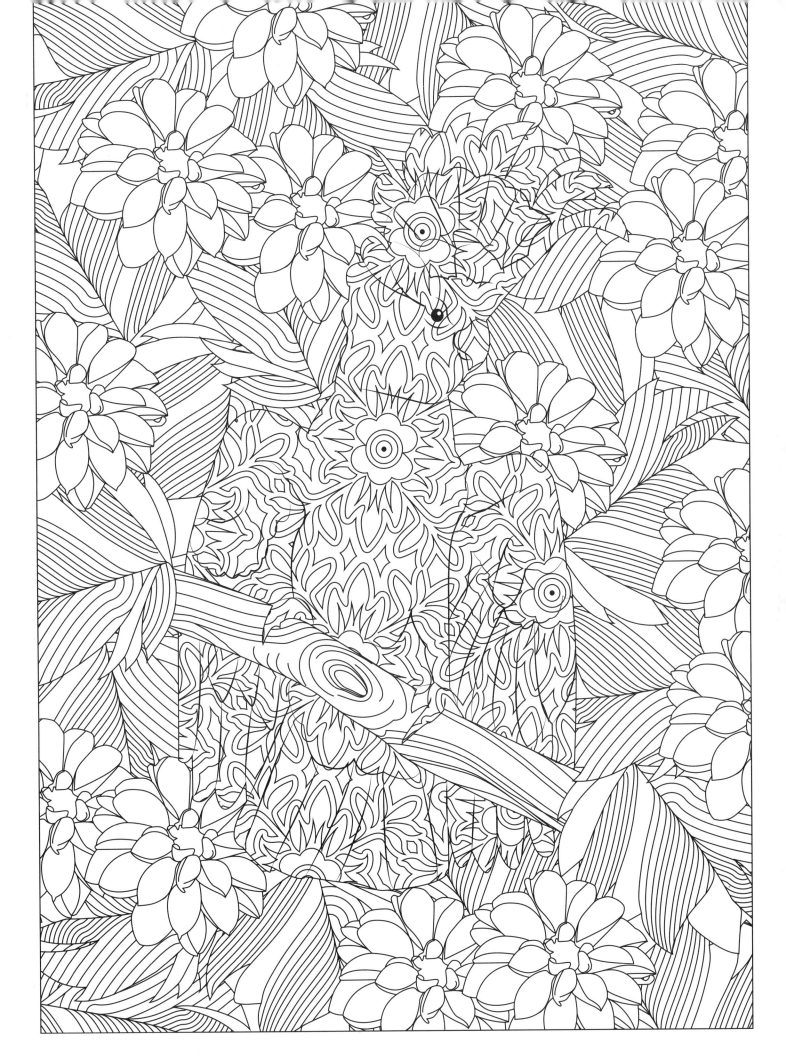

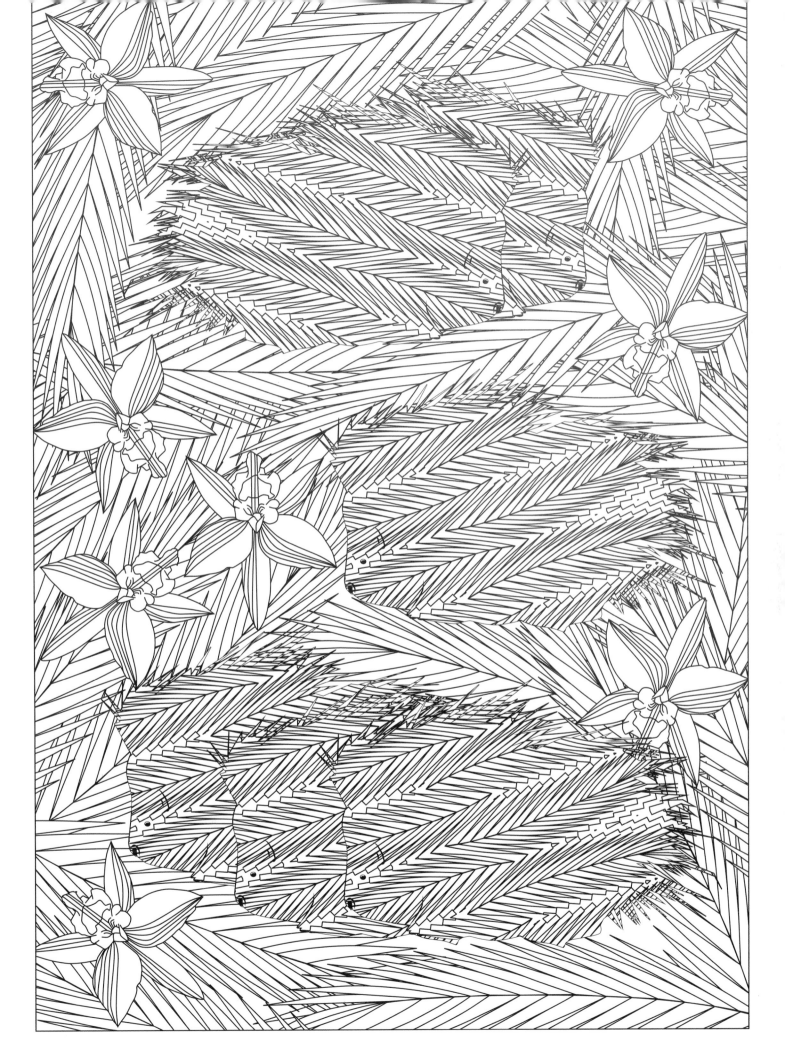

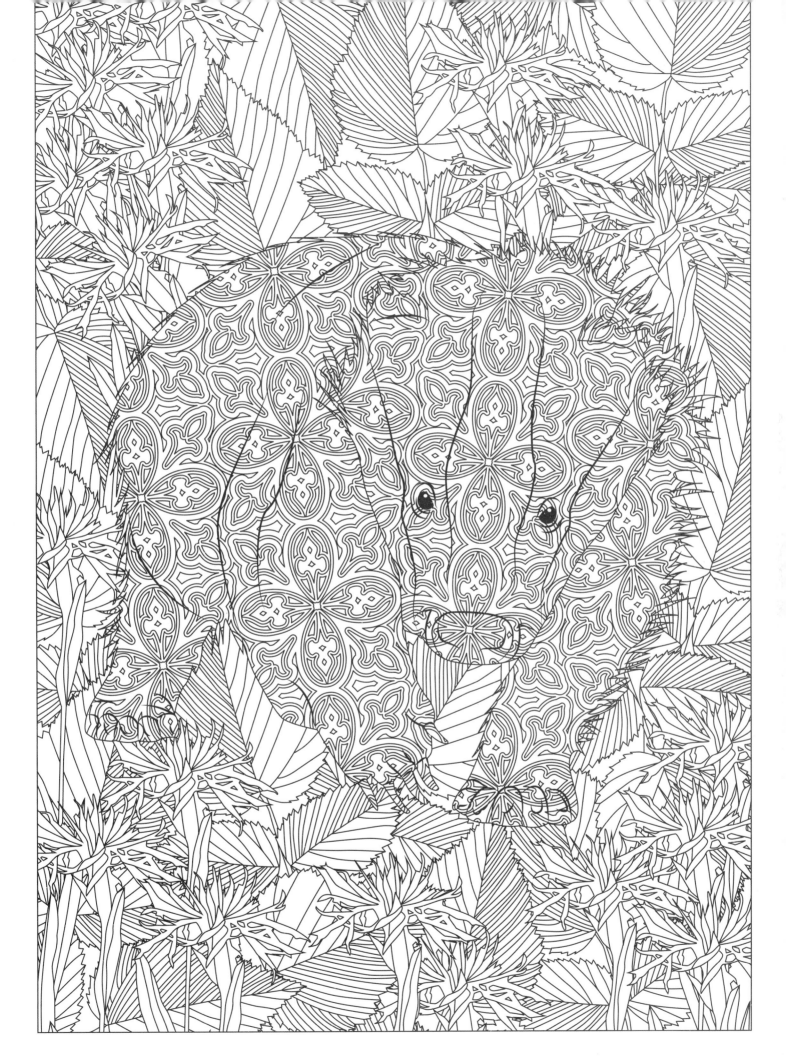

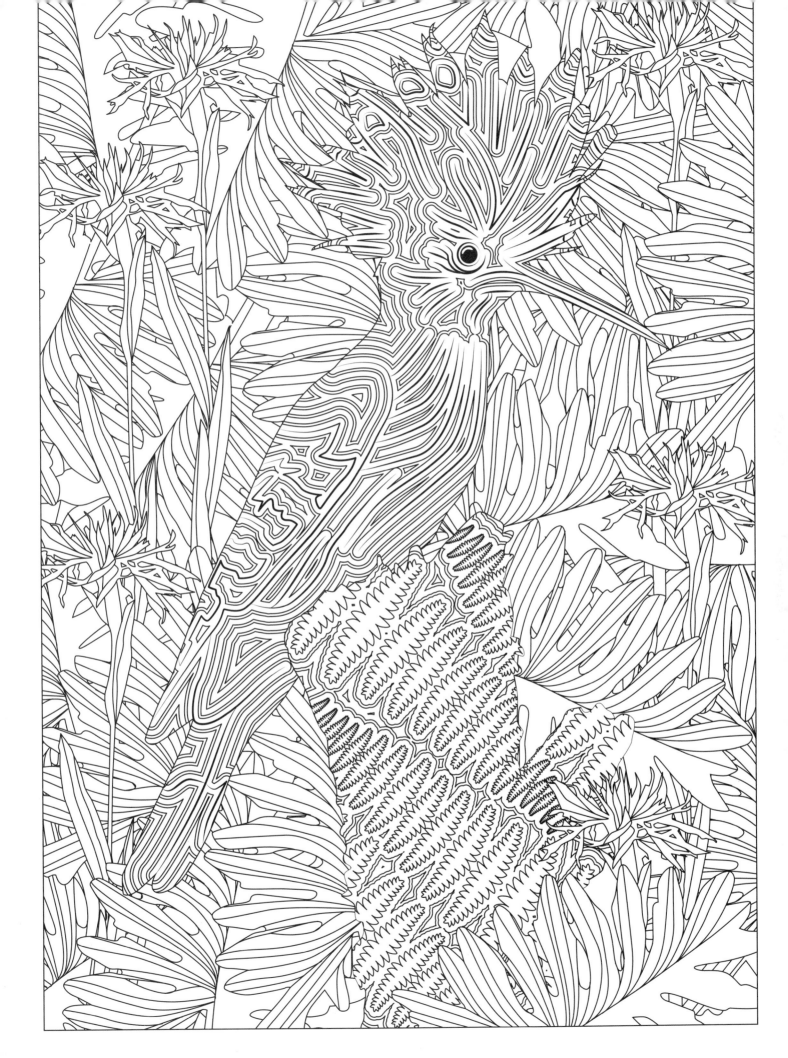

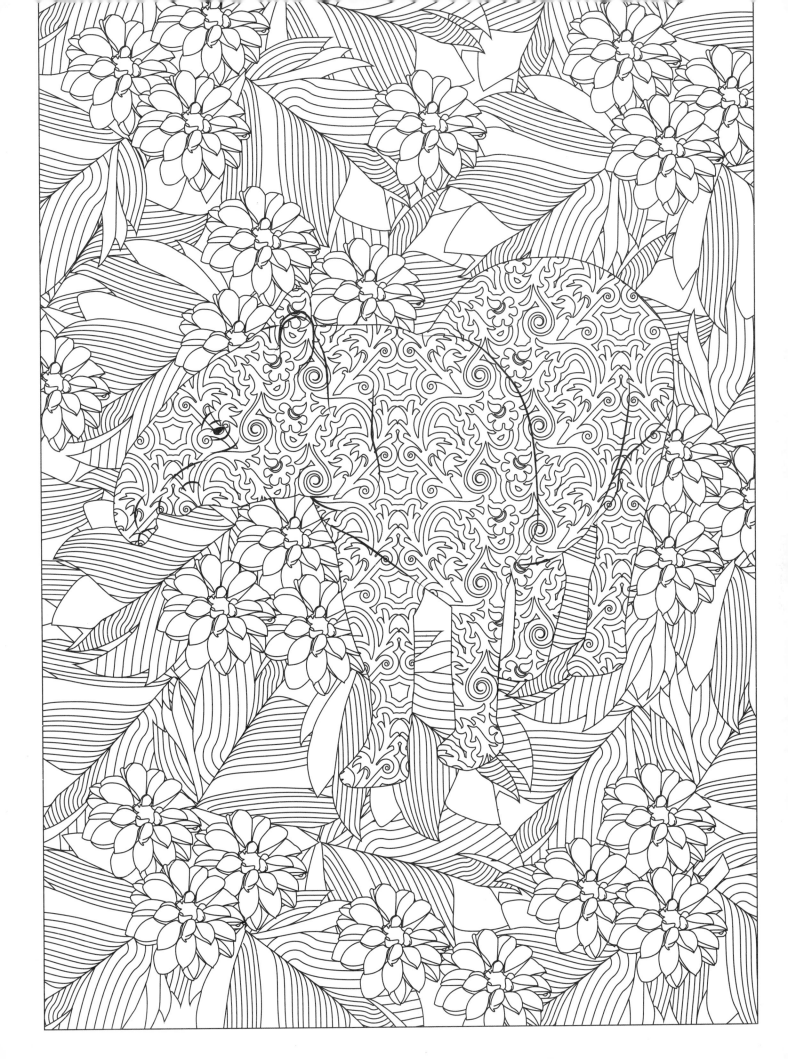

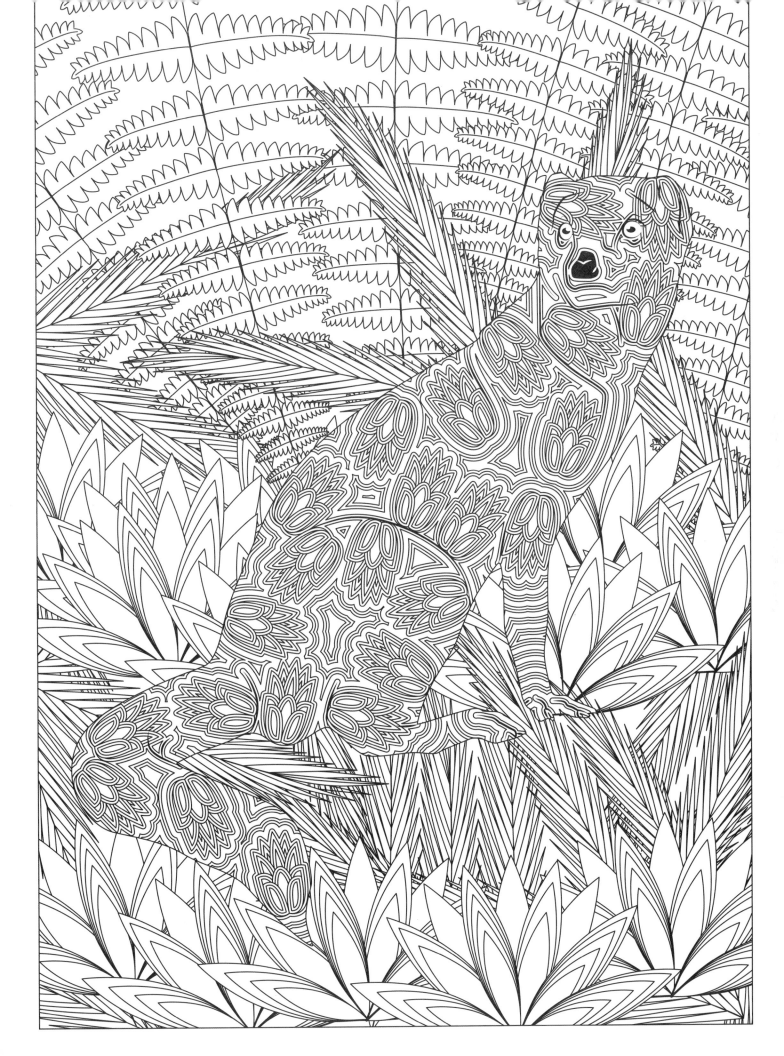

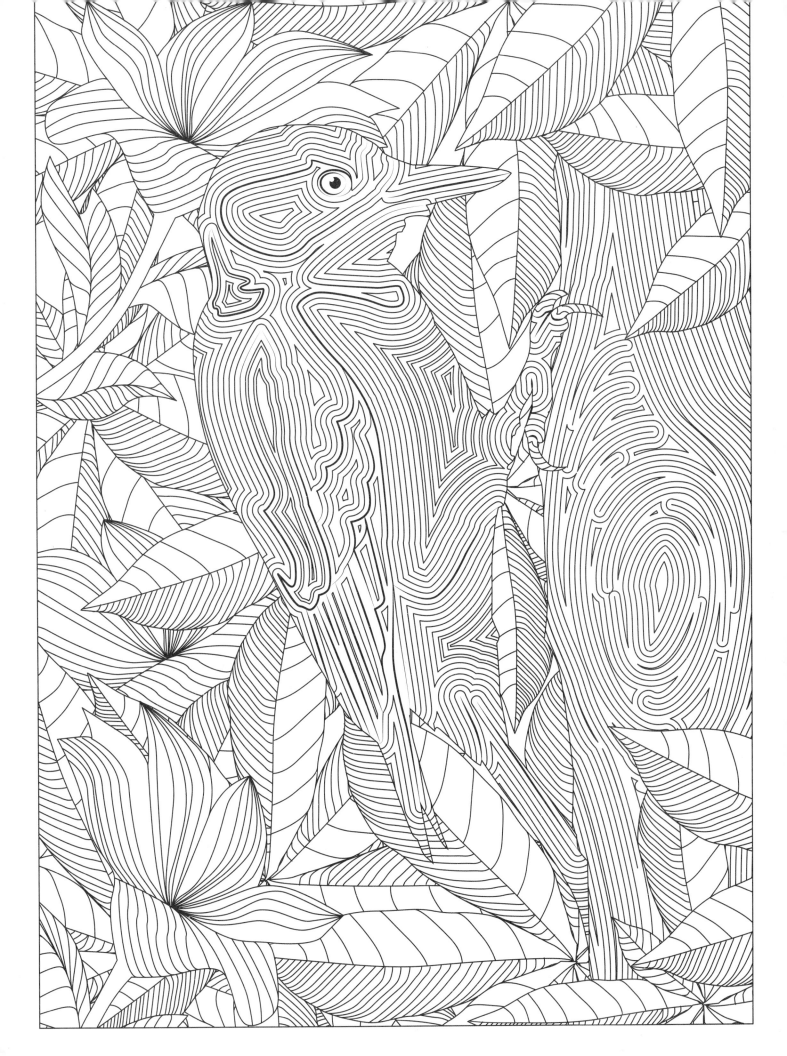

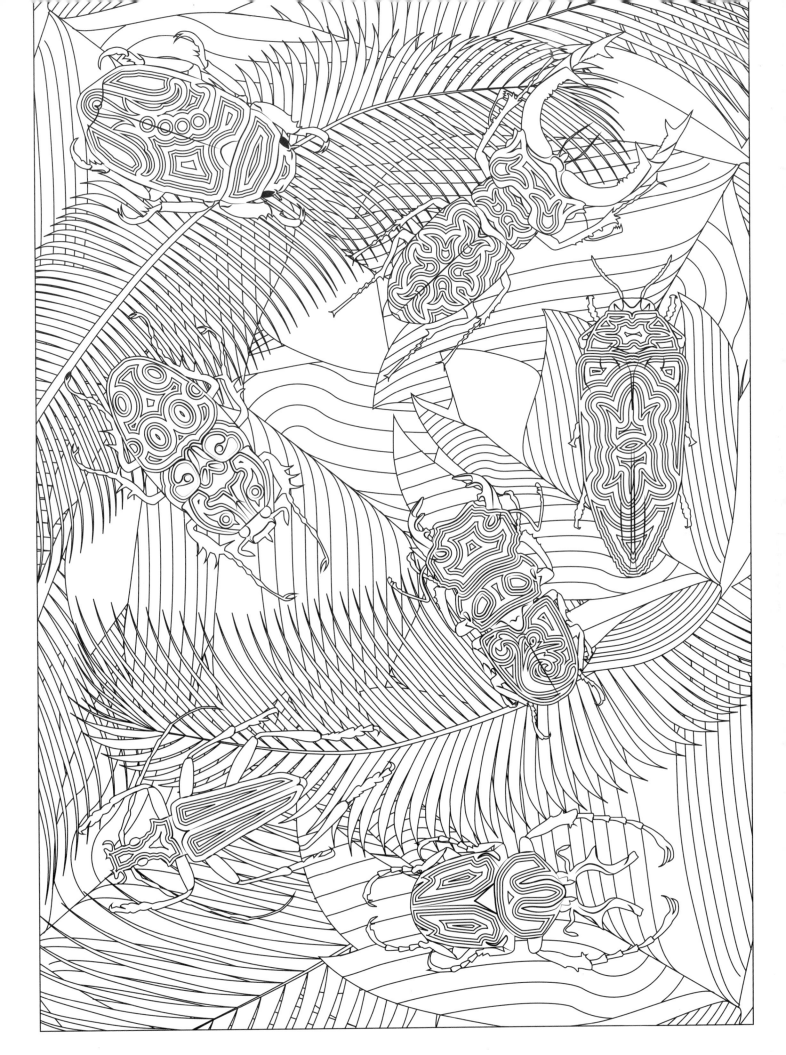

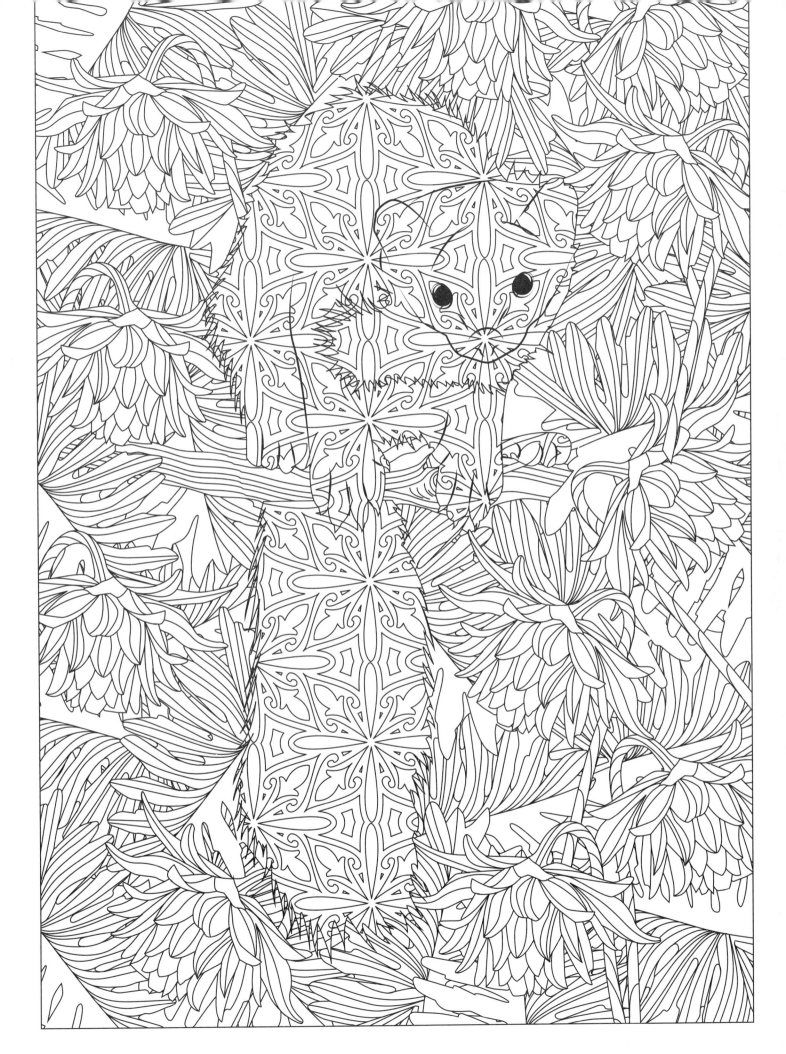

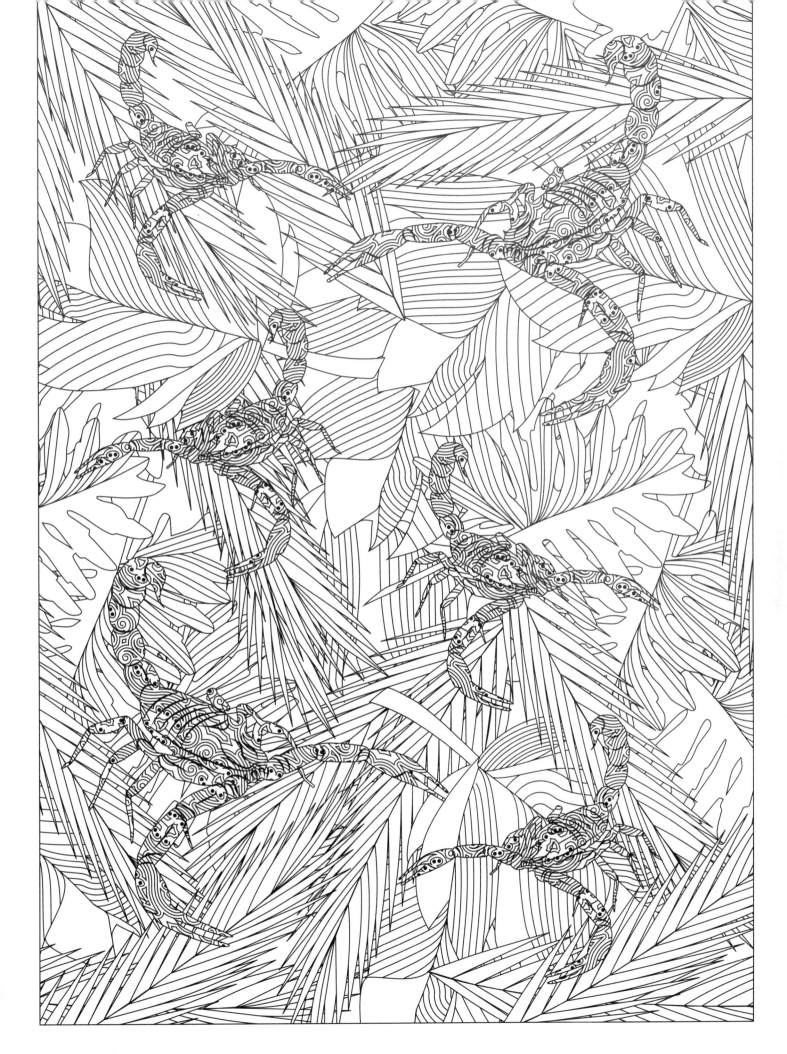

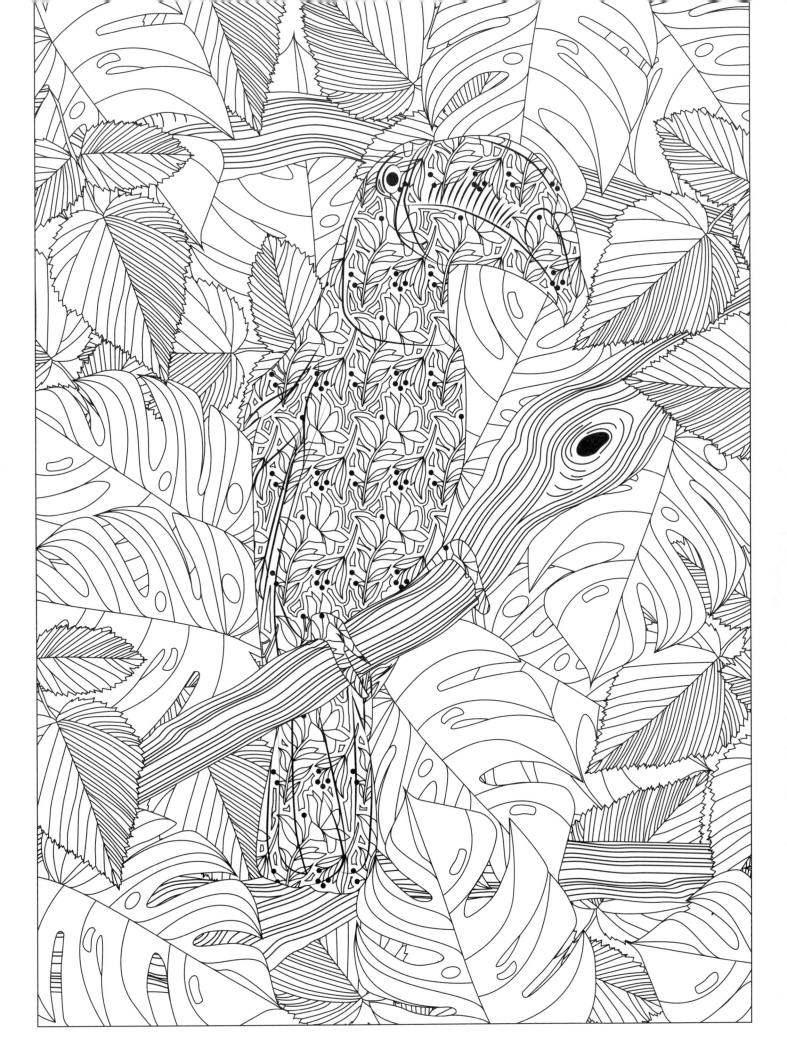

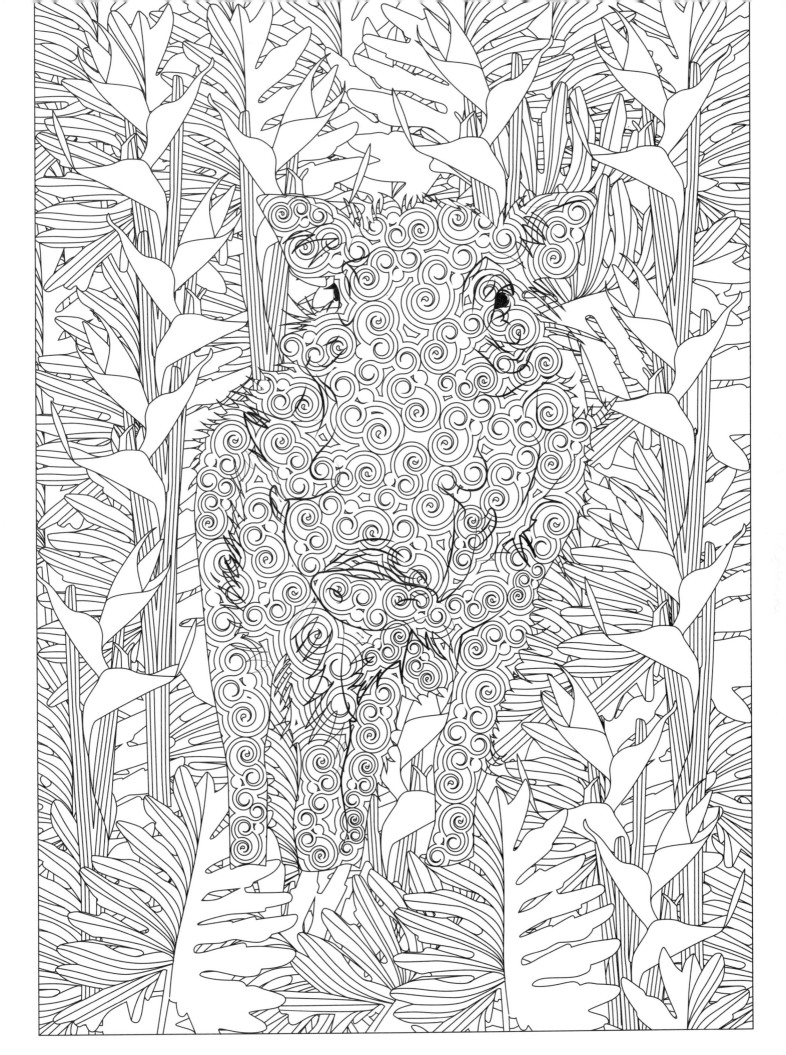

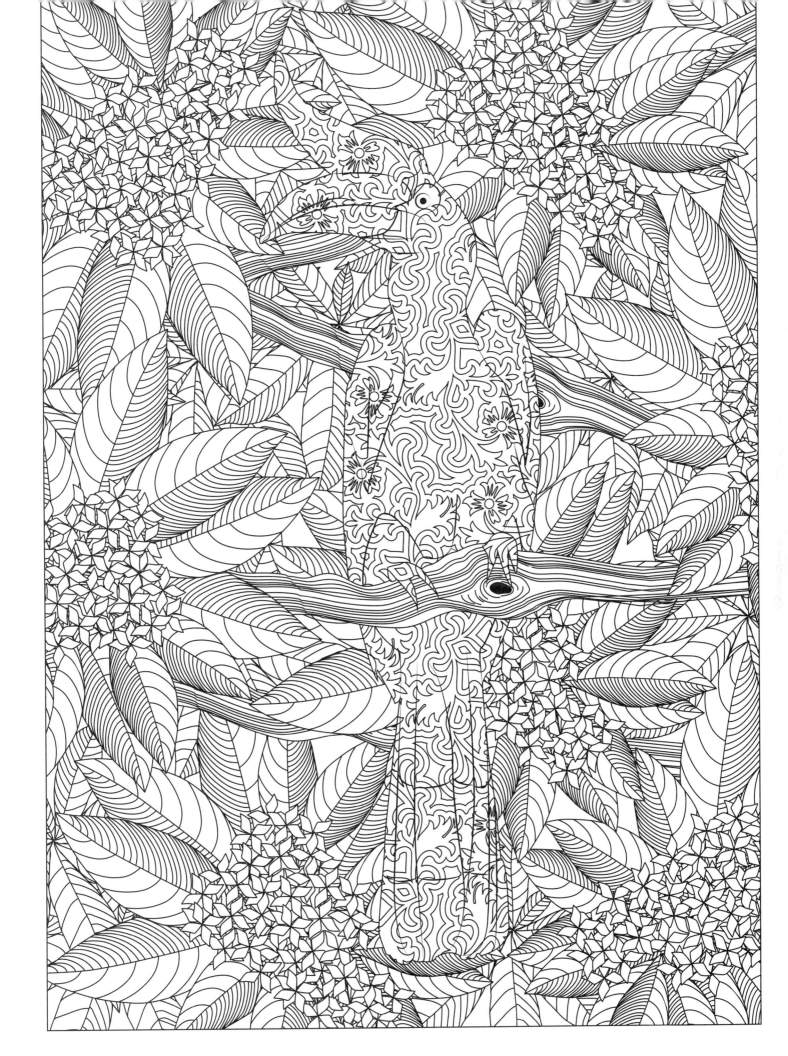

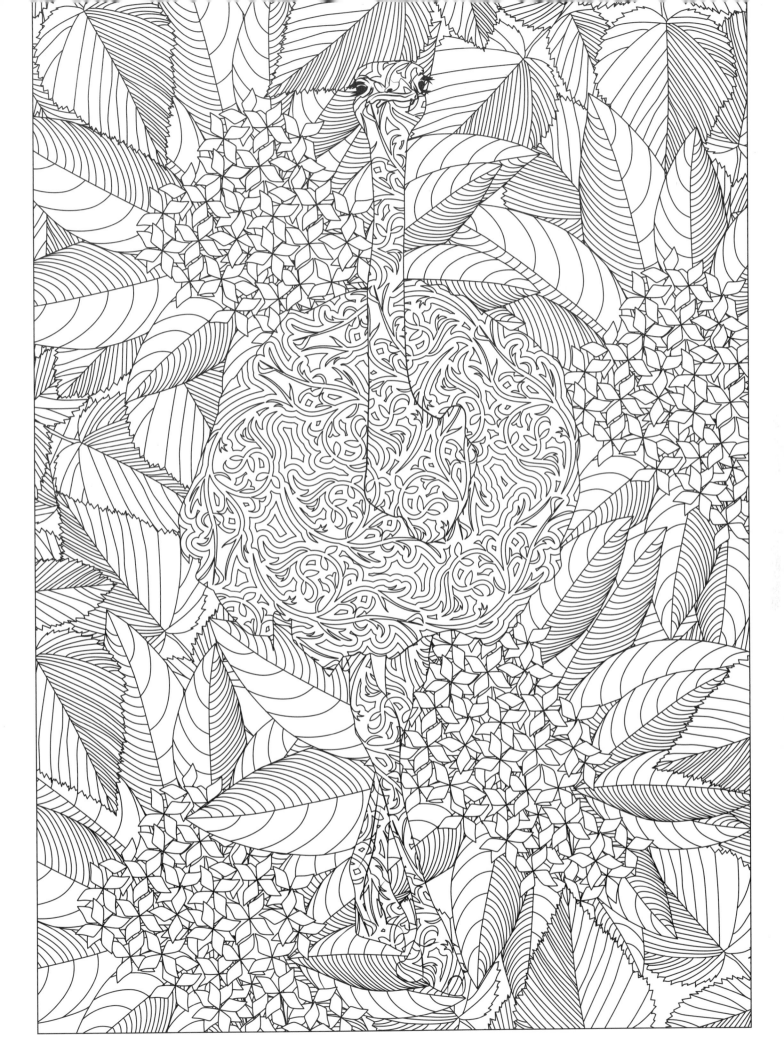

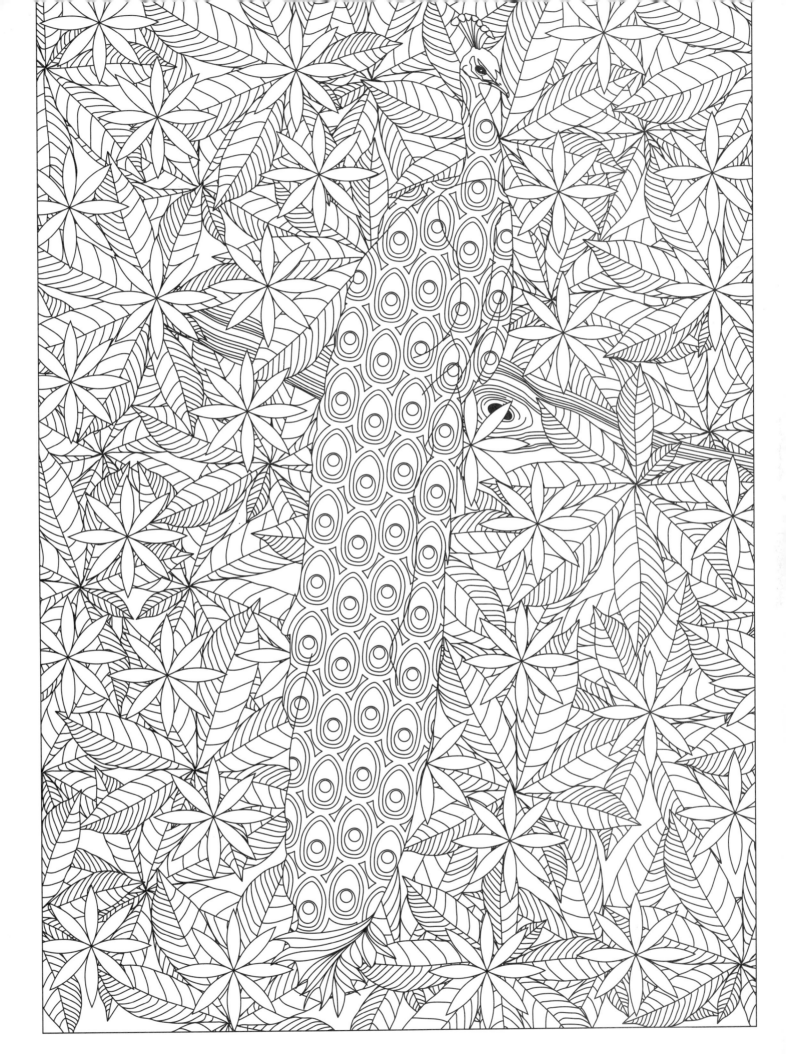

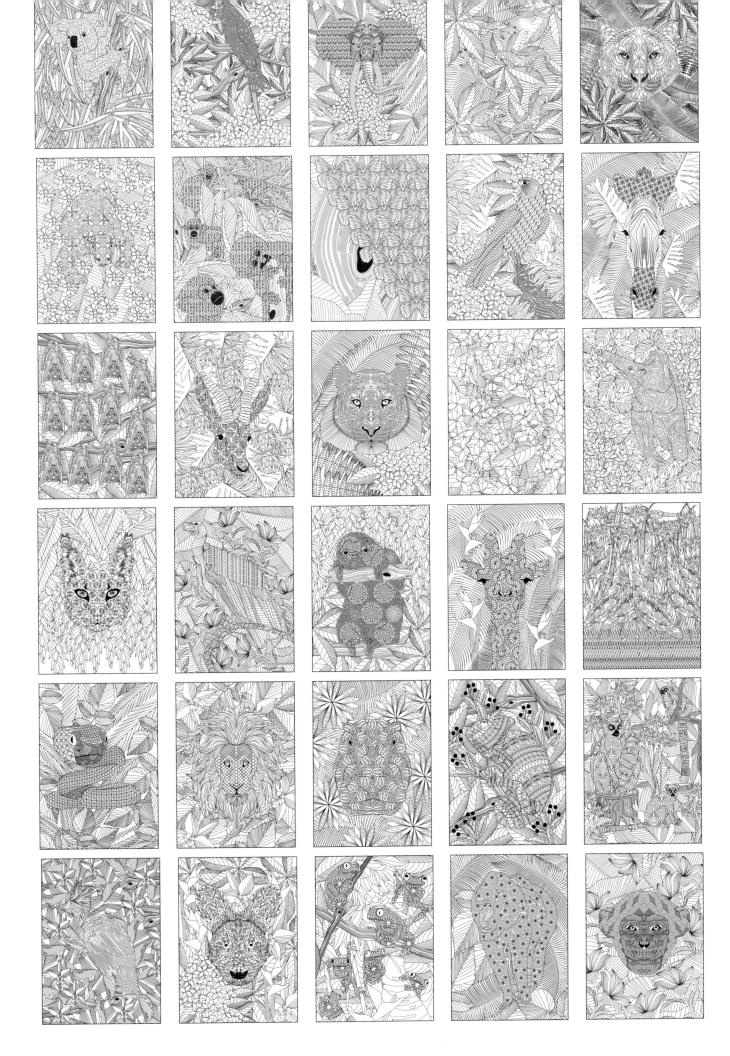

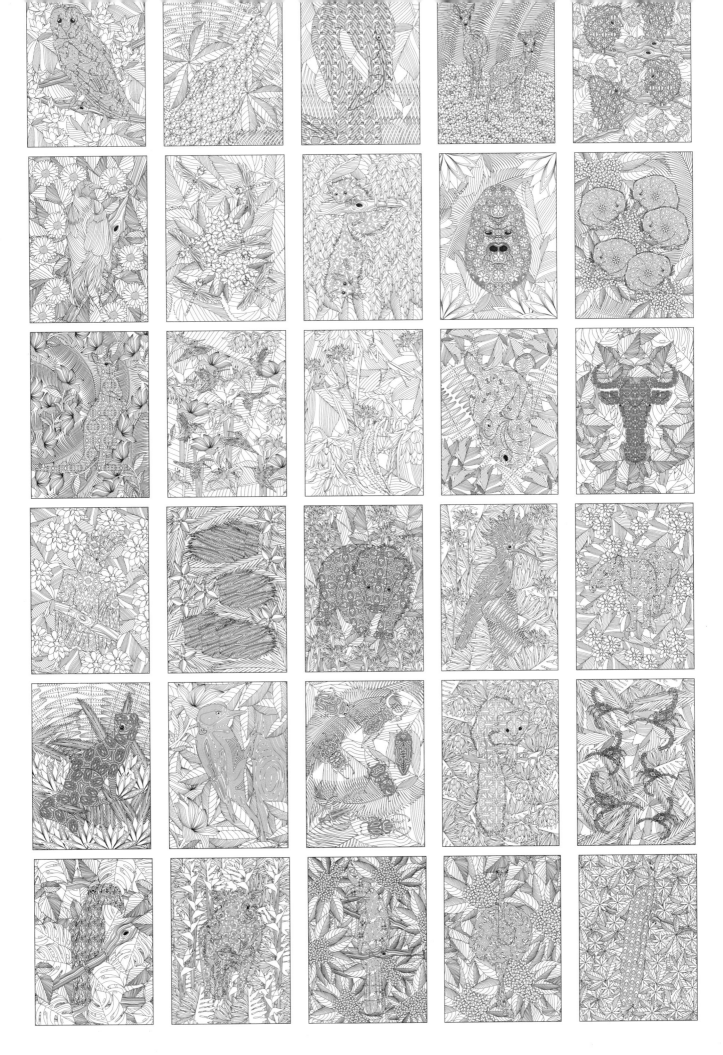